Women
Who Shaped
History

Women
Who Shaped
History

by HENRIETTA BUCKMASTER

COLLIER BOOKS, NEW YORK

COLLIER-MACMILLAN LIMITED, LONDON

FOR MY FRIENDS

Kitty and Carol del Grasso

CONTENTS

INTRODUCTION

This book is about six women who lived in the United States in the nineteenth century—a period of such profound change that a whole new social order was reflected in it.

During the first half of the century slavery grew to monolithic proportions in the agricultural South, while free labor and the expansion of railroads encouraged industrial development in the North. These dual systems led to turmoil and bloodshed even before the Civil War; they also led to powerful protests against the inequalities of the day. Women, for example, had few legal rights; enslaved Negroes had none. Men and women of conscience were increasingly unwilling to tolerate these injustices. Among these dedicated people were six remarkable women, each of whom, in her own way, refused to accept the restrictions established by tradition. As a result, each woman had a marked effect on her own era and the subsequent course of history.

ONE

Dorothea Dix

DOROTHEA DIX was born in Maine in April, 1802. Her childhood was miserable; in later years she never wished to discuss it. But it is probable that she survived that childhood because deep within her were the inherent qualities of determination and compassion.

Her father came from a well-to-do Massachusetts family. He was a student at Harvard when he ran away and married a woman twenty years older than himself. According to the Dix family, she was "poor, ignorant and uncouth." She was apparently no help to her husband or he to her. They had nothing to talk about together and no interests to share.

Shortly after their marriage they moved to a log cabin in Maine, where they tried to farm the harsh land and failed. After the birth of Dorothea and her two brothers, the young father decided to become an itinerant preacher. In many ways this meant an even harsher life for his family. In this wilderness world, itinerant preachers traveled rough forest roads, saw few people, and earned little money. They were often paid in provisions. This meant that when farm yields were poor they might go unpaid and their own families brought close to starvation.

Dorothea and her mother sat hour after hour in the lonely cabin stitching the religious tracts that Joseph Dix sold or exchanged for food.

Dorothea loathed every moment of those wretched silent hours when she cut and folded the printed sermons of her father, pushing a thick needle through the coarse paper in a wearisome effort to keep up with his demands.

At the age of twelve Dorothea rebelled against this dreary life. She ran away to her father's parents in Boston, where she arrived dirty, tired, frightened, and begged to be taken in for ever and ever.

Although the grandparents had disapproved of their son's marriage, Dorothea's grandfather, Dr. Elijah Dix, had occasionally visited them in Maine and had once or twice brought his granddaughter to Boston on a visit. He and the child loved each other.

He welcomed her now. So did her grandmother, but with more reserve. The elder Mrs. Dix had strong convictions of propriety. As far as she was concerned this tall ragged granddaughter needed to be made over in every respect—appearance, manners, education, and, above all, docility.

Their wills clashed.

For two years they clashed so vigorously that at the end of that time Grandmother Dix admitted her failure. Dorothea went to live with a great-aunt in Worcester. At last she was happy.

Here, with a warm, informal family made up of a number of young cousins, Dorothea began to lose her fears and her shyness and some of the black shadows of her childhood which came from privation, loneliness, and lack of love.

Her life was as unresolved as ever, but the problems she now encountered were more manageable. At fourteen she was almost a woman and she knew she must make plans for her future. In 1816 a girl's future was fairly uncomplicated. She had two professions open to her—marriage or teaching.

Dorothea thought constantly about her young brothers and her mother in Maine. If she could earn a living, she could send them occasional gifts of food or clothing. Independence was essential if she were to find herself.

In those days teachers needed few qualifications. Dorothea found a vacant store. She scrubbed the place, brought in benches—with the help of her young cousins—and a desk for herself; she lengthened her skirts and pinned up her hair.

Dorothea was fourteen when she opened her school. She was a strict teacher and disciplinarian. Some of the pain of her own childhood she took out on her pupils. The school became popular, however, and within a short time she had as many as twenty pupils. But at the end of three years, when she was seventeen, she realized how little she knew. She closed her school and returned to her grandparents in Boston. For two years she studied. She studied every book she could borrow. During this time she was so happy that she felt she would like to spend her whole life "living to myself and enjoying literature and art."

But ambition and necessity tugged at her. She was also too vital to lead a solitary life. She had fallen in love with her cousin Edward and promised to marry him—sometime in the future.

In her grandparents' home she opened another school, a far more ambitious one. Here she taught astronomy, minerology, and the natural sciences. Life opened up before her so fully that she hated to waste time even in sleep. She opened a second school for poor children and divided her time between the two. She got up at four in the morning in order to study and to read her Bible. Often she was not in bed until midnight. It is hard to imagine when she had time to see Edward.

Edward waited patiently, hopefully, for a year or so. But it became all too obvious that Dorothea had no time for marriage. The engagement was broken. She gave no reason to her friends. All the letters they had exchanged were burned. She never referred to the engagement in any way.

About this time Dorothea met William Ellery Channing, a great Boston clergyman. He became her friend and the most powerful influence in her life. The doctrine he preached, Sunday after Sunday, was a revolutionary one: "Man must be sacred in man's sight." It was a doctrine of love and compassion. It wiped out forever the merciless doctrine of hopelessness that her father had written into the tracts which she had sewed together so wearily in her childhood.

Dorothea was then nineteen, a tall young woman with great steady eyes and a firm mouth. She wore her dark hair looped low over her ears and caught at the back in a large knot. She was not beautiful but she was attractive with a suggestion of deep-hidden fire. Her intense ambition drove her to constant overwork. At length she collapsed.

The doctor ordered her to bed for a year. Her two schools were closed. But she refused to be defeated and spent the time writing books for children. This was not exactly what her doctor had planned, and he was not surprised that her illness lingered.

The next ten years were spent fighting physical weakness, returning to teaching, collapsing from overwork, and then starting the whole weary round again. She had to battle constantly against her discouragement. If her God wished her to lead a useful life, where was she to find the strength to carry on? To be defeated at thirty was a bitterness she could not bear. Doctor, family, and Dorothea decided—in the fashion of the day—to see if a trip abroad would benefit her. England was her destination.

She arrived in Liverpool so weak from a stormy voyage that she had to be put to bed without delay. Alone and ill in a strange country, her despair reached its lowest point.

Just at that providential moment the Rathbones, Quaker friends of Dr. Channing, called to see her. They recognized the situation at a glance, gathered her up, and took her to their home. Something so bright and strong grew between these three idealistic people that the next eighteen months set the course for Dorothea's whole life.

The Rathbones were vitally concerned with the problems of all mankind, the sick, the poor, the insane. And the most neglected were the insane; they were treated with superstitious brutality or abandoned altogether. A few enlightened doctors were trying to bring some compassion to their care but these doctors were in the minority. One of them was Dr. Samuel Tuke.

Dr. Tuke was in charge of York Retreat, an asylum for the insane supported by the Quakers. It was an amazing institution where an entirely new attitude of love and concern was being used to treat mental disease.

Dorothea met Dr. Tuke, talked with him, and perhaps saw his hospital. In any event by the time she returned to the United States she had been stirred and aroused. It did not seem to occur to her to undertake any similar work for the insane, but she did long to do something equally important.

What could a woman do? A woman with all the handicaps of meager training, all the restrictions laid upon her by society?

Her grandmother, who had died while she was away,

willed her enough money to make her independent. Dorothea knew this money had to be used for some good.
But after a year and a half abroad, on her return to Boston
she found herself a stranger in a strange land. To work
out her destiny was not easy.

She nursed her longing to be truly useful until that
longing had become a bright, steady flame. But her ignorance of social conditions was profound. However, she
knew she wanted no part of the mild, careful, well-super-
vised "good works" of most women.

One day a young man visited her. He was a comparative
stranger. He had come to tell her of the desperate plight
of twenty women prisoners in the Cambridge, Massachusetts, jail. Could Miss Dix suggest some middle-aged lady
who would conduct a Bible class for them on Sundays?

"I'll do it myself," she said.

"But you're too young!" he protested.

She knew she was neither too young nor too old, for
her time of usefulness had arrived. She found the women
as desperate as the young man had described. Among
them were two or three insane prisoners who were
treated even worse than the others, for they were kept
apart and not allowed to share even the meager heat
provided in the bitterly cold winter.

Dorothea discovered to her amazement that she
seemed the only woman in the city appalled by this horror and anxious to do something about it. Her father's religion rose up before her: orthodoxy taught that these
people were sinners being punished. If she had to fight
the whole miserable attitude alone she would do it, for
she was determined that this barbarity must be done to
death.

She was a woman new-made. Dr. Channing's great

theme became hers: Man must be sacred in man's sight. She made an appeal to the jailer and from his apathy received her first lesson in dealing with officials.

From that day on she never thought about her frail health. She went to Dr. Channing for advice. He was dying, but he introduced her to two powerful friends. One was Samuel Gridley Howe, a remarkable Bostonian who had spent his life fighting the cause of forgotten human beings (the deaf and dumb were his special concern). The other was Charles Sumner, who would soon become one of the great champions of Negro rights in the United States.

Both men said that she must have facts, facts, and more facts before anyone could act. For two years she traveled over all of Massachusetts. She visited every jail, almshouse, and workhouse where the indigent insane were kept. She refused to be put off for any cause whatever, sparing herself not a single horror. She took notes on the spot, writing them up in detail when her day was finished. Her travel had to be done by springless stagecoach over roads that were mostly ruts, in bitter winter cold and the terrible heat of summer. The facts that she was gathering should shake the stiffest heart, for the revelations of each new day were more horrifying than the last—the whole experience a nightmare.

At Danvers she heard screams long before she reached the wretched almshouse. In a shed she found a young woman beating on the bars of a cage. She was so filthy that when she scratched at the dirt she tore off her flesh as well. At Little Compton she saw horrors enough but suspected something even worse was being concealed. The jailer's wife hesitated, then said, Wait, she would get a lantern. "Weary and oppressed I leaned against an iron door which closed the sole entrance to a singular stone structure much resembling a tomb," Dorothea wrote of the encounter.

When the door was unlocked, a few steps brought them to a second iron door. When this was opened, Dorothea drew back from the noxious air that poured out.

> Considerable time elapsed before I was able to remain long enough to investigate. The candle illuminated a spectacle never to be forgotten. The place had no light or ventilation. It was about 7 feet by 7, and 6½ feet high. An iron frame interlaced with rope was the sole furniture . . . There he stood near the door, motionless and silent. His tangled hair fell about his shoulders, his bare feet pressed the filthy wet stone floor. He was emaciated to a shadow and more resembled a disinterred corpse than any living creature. I took his hands and endeavored to warm them. I spoke to him of release, of liberty, of care, of kindness. A tear stole over the hollow cheek but no words answered my importunities . . . "My husband," said the woman, "in winter rakes out, sometimes of a morning, half a bushel of frost . . . we have the double walls and two doors because his screams disturb the house."

Her notebooks became volumes. She fought down her horror and went on, for friends were growing. The conscience of many had been roused by the plight of the slave, and when compassion was stirred for any reason it had a way of expanding and including all who were injured. The times were working with Dorothea. But this growing awareness that all individuals had the right to freedom needed friends by the hundreds and thousands.

Three hospitals had already been established in New England to deal humanely with the problems of the insane, but these hospitals had been built and were sustained by courageous individuals without help from the state. The average person did not want to have to think about the misery and agony of strangers.

Dorothea realized that in addition to the facts she had unearthed she must be informed about any practical steps already being taken to ameliorate the situation. She turned to the pioneer doctors who had labored for the hospitals. Dr. Woodward of Worcester Asylum had done the impossible; he had restored sanity to many patients, mostly through love and the expectation of recovery. He and Dr. John S. Butler of the Lunatic Hospital of Boston, and Dr. Luther V. Bell of McLean Hospital in nearby Charlestown were her teachers. All of them believed that decent care, quiet, affection, and normal activity were the only medicine for the insane.

To them, Dorothea and her carefully collected facts were as miraculous as they and their work were to her.

She continued her visits, over and over, to the worst jails and almshouses. Because of her greater professional awareness she saw with even keener eyes. She was careful never to blame the ignorant, underpaid keepers for the conditions, and so she began to gain their cooperation. Slowly it began to dawn on even the dullest of them that cruelty was not a solution to the problem.

Samuel Gridley Howe was now a member of the Massachusetts legislature. He said that as soon as Dorothea had assembled her facts he would present a "memorandum" to his fellow lawmakers.

By 1843 she was ready. She knew she had to present the sickening facts simply, without flourishes. "I proceed, gentlemen, briefly to call your attention to the *present* state of insane persons confined within the Commonwealth, *in cages, closets, cellars, stalls, pens; chained, naked, beaten with rods and lashed into obedience . . ."*

She was strengthened by her knowledge that leading experts in Europe and the United States had practical solutions to offer, and also by the fact that through public education people had been aroused on many other humane subjects.

In June, 1843, Howe rose in the Massachusetts legislature and read aloud Dorothea's report, which presented in vivid detail some of the outrages she had witnessed.

It was an intensely hot day. F was confined in a pen which admitted the scorching rays of the sun. His food was pushed through spaces between the logs. His feet had been frozen by exposure in the winter past. Upon the shapeless stumps, aided by his arms, he raised himself . . . The expedient to prevent him freezing again was strangely horrible. In the center of the pen was excavated a pit six feet square and deep. The top was closed over securely. Into this ghastly place was cast the maniac, there to exist till the returning warm weather. There without heat, without light, without air he was left, whose piteous groans and frantic cries were heard.

Those who detested having such things brought to light raised a great storm of unbelief. Libel suits were threatened, personal attacks on Dorothea flourished like the green bay tree. Her enemies made it seem as though no *decent* lady would allow herself to see and talk about such things; therefore they must be untrue!

Countermemorandums were offered, trying to show that no such conditions existed. But many people were no longer willing to pretend that the world was a perfect place. Dorothea's memorandum was referred to a legislative committee of which Howe was chairman.

The storm increased. The enemies of compassion— all those people who felt that pain and suffering and poverty were sent as punishment by a righteous god and must be endured—joined the enemies of change and developed a quiet ruthless opposition. It was Charles Sumner who came to Dorothea's aid this time. Sumner was young and rich; he was also deeply affected by human suffering. In speech after speech, and in article after article, he set himself to guide public opinion.

In the legislature Dr. Howe waited and watched. At the psychological moment he went to work on his committee, making sure that a favorable bill was reported.

Both Howe and Sumner knew that the public was growing more aware of the rights of men—whether it was the right of the black man to be free of slavery or the right of women to equality or the right of the sick, poor, and insane to public help. The legislators now did not dare openly to oppose a bill, although many, in secret, tried to kill it. On the day that the bill was put to a vote, Dorothea waited at a friend's house during the anxious hours. Even now it might be defeated on a technicality. But Howe brought her the triumphant word that it had passed by a large majority.

Now Massachusetts hospitals would be compelled to enlarge their facilities to include special sections for the most modern care of the insane.

From this day, Dorothea did not question the direction of her future. Between June, 1843, and August, 1847, she traveled thirty thousand miles. She went from Canada to the Gulf of Mexico, from the Atlantic to the Mississippi River, in the great cause of arousing public compassion and responsibility. Every state in the Union had to be wakened.

From a doctor's point of view she was a chronic invalid.

From her point of view nothing could stop her. Her course was so well plotted, her techniques so sure, that she had the courage to take one step at a time. She relaxed by making little gifts, small inconsequential things, to give to some shattered old man or raving young woman as a gesture of loving concern. This loving concern was, she knew, a very important remedy.

Apathy, political expediency, and greed were her greatest enemies. Dorothea was often discouraged. Because she was a woman she was prevented from taking direct action. She always had to work through a man. Fortunately she invariably found a humane, farsighted man anxious to further her work.

These men admired her calmness and courage—and worried about her. One such man wrote to a friend: "Miss Dix has been with us and leaves us tomorrow. She is greatly exhausted and I fear to hear that she has succumbed somewhere in a lonely place. What a heroine she is! I have the highest veneration for her heart and head."

Well he might! There were few men—and few women either—who could have lived the life that circumstances forced upon Dorothea. Sometimes she felt as though her home was a stagecoach, a cart, a lumber wagon—anything that would move along roads that scarcely existed. "I crossed the Yadkin where it was three-quarters of a mile wide, the water always up to the bed of the carriage and sometimes seeping in. The horses rested twice on sand bars . . . A few miles beyond river, the axletrees of the carriage broke and away rolled one of the back wheels."

The breakdowns were so frequent, the delays so agonizing, that she got in the habit of including a repair kit in her luggage: grease, nails, tools, rope. While the driver used her tools for repairs, she would sit on a tree stump or a rock, bonneted and shawled, writing, writing, writing. Her voluminous skirts were spread about her, for she must present a picture of unfailing respectability.

Traveling down the Mississippi, cholera and scarlet fever broke out on the boat. She nursed the sick, though she herself became ill. "Up again from malarial fever," she wrote a friend. "Off to Jackson, Mississippi, tonight."

Sometimes the physical hardships must have seemed inconsequential compared to the spiritual agonies she went through trying to persuade a hard, money-minded legislator that human suffering was his responsibility. She who had seen horror in its most appalling guises— had seen men and women buried alive—had to learn how to speak unemotionally and reply patiently to cruel questions.

She drew her strength from success. In Rhode Island she persuaded a rich man to build a hospital for the insane. In New Jersey her "first-born child," as she called it, came into existence: a state hospital in which all the citizens of New Jersey, not merely one humane millionaire, were involved.

But each success was the result of visiting every poorhouse and every jail in a state, of endless hours of argument, of patient infuriating work behind the scenes; for, as a woman, she could never make speeches, never thrust herself forward. She grew weary unto death of having to go over the same ground dozens and dozens of wearisome times, of having to answer with a patience she could hardly endure the same trite and brutal objections.

She allowed herself, however, one flat undebatable statement. "Sir," she would say, "I have not come to ask any favor for myself. I ask for *yourself*, your state, your people."

Gradually she became famous. She had a remarkable gift for sizing up people and for making friends with men of influence. In the South she found it necessary to avoid the question of slavery and to appeal to men's chivalry . . . she a helpless white lady of such gentility!

By 1848 enough states had responded to the facts she presented for Dorothea to tackle the biggest job of all—the Federal Government.

Public land, selling for $1.25 an acre, cried out to be used for public good. She made an appeal for a Federal appropriation of five million acres to be turned into a fund to aid the poor and neglected insane.

In many ways it was a very daring move. Railroads coveted this land and were willing to pay $2.50 an acre or more. She had many friends among the congressmen. She worked with them so closely that a special alcove in the Capitol library was set aside for her use, where she could meet with them daily.

The bill was presented to a select committee and was reported back favorably. By now she knew so well how politicians worked that she curbed her optimism. She was not surprised or even bitterly disappointed when the bill was deferred.

She must simply enlarge its objectives! She must ask for *more* land and include the deaf and dumb in the bill's provisions! She left Washington to build up, single-handed, the support that her congressmen would need.

She went to churches: they must exert pressures. She went to doctors, that is, to the small handful of medical pioneers, the superintendents of the new institutions for the insane, which she had been sowing behind her as fast as she could move. They must give unqualified support.

There is no question that Dorothea and the age in which she lived worked together. Appeal to the conscience, and you appealed to something almost organic in its response. Probably the terrible unresolved pall of slavery, now reaching a climax, had a great deal to do with the problems of guilt and response.

Her exhaustion must have been almost unendurable sometimes, knowing as she did that the protests of her opponents were becoming mechanical and yet must be answered with the same old tedious painstaking care.

In February, 1851, the bill came up in the Senate. She and friends in Congress held their breath. It was passed by a large majority. Dorothea almost collapsed from relief.

Yet she knew that this was not the end of the road— not by any means. With bitter irony, Congress adjourned before the House could act on the bill. This meant the whole business of introducing a bill had to be gone through again.

When Congress reconvened, petitions and letters supporting the bill poured into the congressmen's offices. Newspapers wrote glowing editorials. The Senate passed it by a large vote. The House almost tripped over itself to do the same.

Now she could sign with relief, for the new President, Franklin Pierce, whose signature was needed, was an old friend of Dorothea's. He had shown his interest in unmistakable ways.

It was this old friend, trusted Franklin Pierce, who vetoed the bill.

The shock was incalculable.

In his veto message President Pierce claimed that every

human weakness or sorrow would take advantage of this bill if it became law. He said it endangered states' rights. He said he was forced to veto it in order "to resist the deep sympathies of my own heart."

Congressional indignation did not sway him. And many who had voted for the bill were caught in the expedient ebb of hard politics and refused to vote against his veto.

The shock for Dorothea was almost more than she could bear. All she could remember was the endless work, the exhaustion, the thirty thousand miles she had traveled. A Congressional bill was now out of the question for many years. Washington could hear nothing but the rising clamor between North and South on the issue of slavery.

It was impossible for Dorothea to give up hope so abruptly. She would have died in her tracks! Friends urged her to go abroad, to study the situation there. She did. She found a new life.

In Scotland, she, a stranger, raised such a commotion over the conditions of the insane that Parliament was forced by public opinion to authorize a royal commissioner for Scotland who would be responsible for improving the condition of the insane in that country.

Although forced to spend half of each week in bed, Dorothea set out for France. Once more she was the right person at the right time. Her technique for assembling facts, her skill in presenting them, flung open doors that were already slightly ajar. Although she spoke only the most rudimentary French, she was authorized to enter any prison or hospital of Paris.

She traveled through Europe as she had traveled through the United States, looking for the same facts. When she finally returned home she had gained perspective. She saw that the momentum of deepening con-cern made future changes inevitable. In Vienna new at-tention was being paid to the emotional nature of mental ills. In Turkey and Russia far more imaginative care had been developed than in all western Europe. Fresh winds were blowing everywhere.

Long experience had taught her that such freshened points of view were needed almost more than hospitals, although hospitals were burgeoning in the United States: more than one hundred had been newly estab-lished in ten years' time.

Each new hospital proved that proper nursing was al-most as important for mental patients as proper doctoring. At that time nursing was almost a disreputable occupa-tion, and decent women kept away from it. Uneducated, crude, often cruel, women took up "nursing."

Dorothea spent the next four years doing an amazing job of educating women, and the public in general, to al-most every aspect of hospital care. She was, in a very real sense, "ready" when the Civil War broke out.

Ready perhaps in more ways than one. One of her friends was Samuel Fenton, president of the Philadel-phia and Baltimore Railroad. Abraham Lincoln was on his way from Illinois to Washington for his inauguration and Mr. Fenton was responsible for the last stage of the journey. The entire country was tense; the threat of war hung over every town and village. Southern extremists were calling Lincoln their greatest enemy and the men responsible for Lincoln's safety feared an eruption of vio-lence when they reached the southern state of Mary-land. While Lincoln's train was still in New York State Mr. Fenton received a message that his friend Dorothea Dix wished to see him urgently and privately.

They were closeted for more than an hour. When Mr. Fenton emerged he sent a whole series of urgent telegrams. Private detectives answered his summons, and Lincoln, to his astonishment, was taken off the train and smuggled into Washington—"disguised," rumor said.

It seems that Dorothea on her last trip to the South had accumulated some startling evidence that Southern slaveowners planned to move on Washington, seize the government, and stop the inauguration of Lincoln by assassination if necessary. Some of the evidence was solid fact, some was wild fancy, but Dorothea's reputation for scrupulous reporting alerted the Secret Service and brought her profuse thanks from the government.

When the first battle of the Civil War revealed the total inadequacy of any field care for the wounded, Dorothea knew she had to strike out for an unpopular cause: nursing care for the soldiers. She was worn, anxious, an elderly woman, but she knew this task was imperative.

In previous wars the wounded were cared for by companions as best they could. At the outbreak of the Civil War there were few Army doctors. Hygiene was virtually nonexistent, and more died from infection than from their original injuries. Hospital care and nursing for the wounded was unknown, although Florence Nightingale in England was storming officialdom to obtain reforms.

During the summer of 1861 Dorothea went to the War Office. She was so well known in Washington that she was able to get quick action on her offer to establish a woman's volunteer nursing corps. The army opposed it, but the civilian authorities in the war department accepted readily.

Dorothea's life for the next four years deserves a story to itself. Doctors resisted virtually every move she made.

Her supporters could be counted on one hand. The extent of red-tape opposition to the care of the wounded is almost impossible to comprehend today. Dorothea fought apathy, antagonism, and even some of the women volunteers who, she felt, were more concerned with personal comfort than with providing proper nursing care. She also had to fight *for* everything. The barest minimum of supplies were available. She had to raise the money for swabs and bandages. Yet she got things done, forcefully demanding action when requests were ignored or delayed. By now she was too sick and tired to act politicly. She lost her temper again and again. She did not care whose toes she stepped on. She demanded court-martialing for every doctor found drunk. She took straight up to the Secretary of War every case of carelessness to a wounded soldier.

But red tape and hostility nearly defeated her spirit before the war was over. After the war she returned thankfully to the easy task of caring for the insane. By this time she had the satisfaction of knowing that her work was honored from one end of the country to the other. Each hospital she visited was "hers."

When she was seventy-three she watched a class of nurses graduate, the first class in the world especially trained for the care of the insane. She watched with tears in her eyes.

She died within the walls of that New Jersey hospital she called her "first born." She was still planning what she would do next.

A doctor spoke her epitaph. "She was the most useful and distinguished woman America has yet produced."

Prudence Crandall

P RUDENCE CRANDALL was born in Connecticut in 1803. Her parents were Quakers and instilled in her a sense of responsibility to any who needed her help. This attitude of usefulness was an essential part of a Quaker upbringing. The Quakers set themselves, in a gentle way, against conventional attitudes of both church and society if the welfare of men or women was the issue. Conscience was their guide.

Since teaching was one of the few professions open to women, Prudence opened a school in her home town of Plainfield, but after a few months she heard of an opportunity to open a larger school in Canterbury, Connecticut.

Canterbury was a prosperous town, and the well-to-do citizens felt the need of an adequate school for their daughters. The district school taught only reading, writing, and arithmetic, but rich men's daughters must know how to sew, draw, play the piano, and have all the polished graces that money could buy.

Prudence came to Canterbury in her modest Quaker gown and shawl to discuss the matter. Several fathers were willing to advance the money for a proper school; her own father was willing to invest his savings. Miss Crandall, tall, slender, attractive, and genteel, was obviously just the right person.

A house was rented on the village green. There was a great bustle of painting and scrubbing. Curtains were sewed, carpets swept, desks and books bought; and in the fall of 1831 Prudence stood in the door and welcomed her first students.

She must have looked at these girls with love and pride. She wanted to give them the best she knew. She watched their faces as she read aloud the rules of the school: "Never tell a lie or use artful evasion, nor wrong any person by word or deed. Mock not the aged, the lame, the deformed, or insane, or any other person. Throw no sticks, stones, dirt, snowballs, or any other thing at any person or any creature. Never return an injury or affront, but forgive. In all things, to all people, behave in a modest and civil manner. Courteously use the word 'please' or some soft expression when you ask anything, one of the other. The objects of education are twofold: mental development and knowledge of facts useful in life."

This was a high and exact standard. But the girls did not look dismayed. As the weeks went on Prudence had every reason to feel that she had found her purpose and reason in life.

Her sister, Almira, helped with the teaching and a young colored girl named Marcia acted as housekeeper. Marcia had lived with the Crandalls all her life. She was now seventeen and had recently become engaged to a young man named Charles Harris. Charles had a sister, Sarah. Sarah wanted an education.

Slavery had been abolished in Connecticut in 1784. Negroes were permitted to own land and send their children to the district schools. But that was about all the freedom they had. "Black laws" restricted them in almost every other way.

Most white people felt that Negroes should be kept as low as possible. When Sarah asked Prudence to teach her, Prudence put her off with friendly words. She might believe that all men were equal in the sight of God, but one was also cautious when an investment was at stake. Yet Prudence discovered she was having trouble with her conscience.

In this year, 1831, prosperity and peace were inextricably linked to slavery by many politicians and businessmen. Slavery might horrify people, but it was so far away, stretching from Delaware to Texas, that the average northerner could ignore its implications. Slavery had been abolished in the Northern States, and business with the South was so flourishing that only a fool would stir up trouble.

In Canterbury, Prudence's students were happy and their parents were pleased. As the lovely young girls went on their daily walk in the sunlight, two by two, fathers and mothers congratulated themselves on the good fortune that had brought Miss Crandall to Canterbury.

And Prudence congratulated herself and would have been quite content if only Sarah's face had not risen up before her so often.

In Boston sounds of antislavery protest were being heard. They were faint sounds, nothing to challenge the mighty power of slavery, coming from a small newspaper called *The Liberator*, edited by a man named William Lloyd Garrison. It attracted barely a handful of readers who were already convinced of its message: SLAVERY MUST GO!

But Garrison was a brilliant editor. He had a breathtaking way of stating his convictions and offering his evidence. *The Liberator* was stirring up a reaction far greater than the circulation of the paper would seem to justify.

A year passed. Prudence's pretty school on the village green was as much a part of the town as the Congregational Church. How a copy of *The Liberator* ever came into Prudence's hands we will never know. But the day she picked it up and read the first lines was a day that changed her life.

All through the night she struggled with her conscience. The hours seemed endless. She had been raised to follow where her conscience led her. All good people denounced enslavement. What had she done to open a door? She had even refused the small thing that had been asked of her—a colored girl's chance of a better education.

In the blackness of the night she saw her reason. For years she had pretended to be completely free of prejudice, but now she admitted to herself that the sight of a dark-skinned person roused a deep distaste. This new awareness shocked her.

She took up her Bible and read again that God had created all nations of the earth.

When daylight came Prudence felt as though she had been washed clean. She called Sarah to her and said, "Last night a war went on in my soul, and I could find no rest. But today I stand on the side of victory, and rest will come in its time."

Sarah should receive the education she wished. It was her right.

Sarah was overjoyed. Her father was as delighted as Sarah and said he would pay her full tuition just as the other fathers did. Prudence agreed, for she knew the self-respect which came from being treated without discrimination was just as important as the education.

Almira, Prudence's sister, was not as pleased as the

others. She foresaw trouble. Shouldn't Prudence talk over her decision with some of the other students' fathers, such as Mr. Andrew Judson or Mr. Richard Fenner?

Prudence shook her head. She said that Sarah had gone to the district school with the very girls she would now be studying with. They were kind, courteous girls who had lived scrupulously by the rules of the school.

Perhaps Prudence was a little frightened. She knew she dared not let herself think too long about her decision. The next day Sarah Harris, in a plain brown dress, sat down beside a white girl student.

Prudence watched. She saw the quick looks that passed from girl to girl. She observed Sarah's quiet, unruffled manner. She saw one or two of the white girls flush and bite their lips. When she began the recitation, one student burst into tears.

Prudence took out the rules of the school and read them aloud slowly and without comment: Harm no one . . . behave courteously . . . forgive all.

The next day was Sunday. As usual Prudence, Almira, and Marcia went to church.

Not a single person spoke to them.

That evening Mr. Andrew Judson came to see Prudence. Mr. Judson had invested the largest sum of money in the school. His daughter was a pupil. He was president of the Canterbury Colonization Society, which believed that all Negroes should be shipped back to Africa.

He got to his point quickly. A colored girl had been given equality with his daughter; he was insulted. Other fathers were outraged. Prudence answered that God had given Sarah her color and what God gives He gives in trust. "I respect black as I do white."

This was no answer as far as Mr. Judson was concerned.

Prudence refused to be moved. She repeated that as a Quaker she accepted the principle of universal brotherhood.

Mr. Judson was by now growing angry. He said that both church and society had decided that Negroes were incapable of rising above a menial position, and he would see that they were prevented from any attempt! If Sarah were not removed from the school immediately, the school would be closed.

He left Prudence to think this over. The next morning Sarah was again in the class. That evening another father rang the doorbell. Richard Fenner, a storekeeper, was calmer but just as insistent. He said that higher education for Negroes made them dangerous. He impatiently brushed aside Prudence's moral arguments.

Prudence drew a deep breath. "I buy provisions for thirty people. I buy them from your store, Mr. Fenner. I spend a great deal of money in your store. Is this fact not of some interest to you?"

Mr. Fenner fumbled for words. His aggressiveness became mixed with confusion. He left abruptly.

The next day two mothers arrived. By now Prudence was fully aware that her only hope lay in holding her course. She told the mothers that even if the school was threatened with closure she would not dismiss Sarah.

When Judson returned for her decision, she told him Sarah would continue as her pupil. He looked at her craftily. "To fail at your age—if you will pardon my mentioning so delicate a matter—could ruin your life."

Prudence was thirty and she acknowledged his point. "But I shall not fail."

He replied, "It is now a question of twenty-four white students or one black."

As Judson knew, this school meant everything to Prudence. She was deeply unhappy. She decided to talk to the man whose ideas had precipitated the crisis. She went to Boston to see Garrison.

She had never met him, but the two, facing each other in a hotel lobby, must have recognized kindred souls. She was tall and slender, not beautiful but very attractive; he was tall, spare, not handsome but with an expression as alert and intelligent as a hawk. Neither could live serenely if their consciences were twisted awry —if they sacrificed a sense of right to any expediency.

She told Garrison she could not deny Sarah an education. This meant she was prepared to devote her whole future to Negro students. All her hopes, all the money her father could spare, had been invested in the Canterbury school. She could not afford to fail in her dream of being an educator. If Negroes were to be her students, all the better.

He warned her, "If the admission of one colored student to your school has caused trouble, the trouble may multiply as you add more."

"I do not think so, Mr. Garrison. If I close the school completely to white students, what fear can there be?"

He smiled at her. "The school that seems small to you may prove to be the spark that will ignite a flame of feeling." After all, her enemies could not afford to have their theories of inferiority proved baseless. "All the forces of darkness will try to stamp you out if you knock away one of the strongest props of slavery."

He warned her well and conscientiously, which merely strenghtened her determination to devote her school to

Negro students. He then ceased to warn her and gave her moral strength.

"Remember, Miss Crandall, two million Negroes are still in subjection. If denied the right to education, what other rights may not be denied them?" He took her hand. "The cause of free men everywhere demands that you accept the challenge."

He provided her with the names of Negro and white antislavery families in Boston, Providence, New Haven, and Philadelphia who would give her money and moral support.

She promptly called on the Boston families, and then set out for New York and Philadelphia. In Canterbury the classes went on with Almira teaching.

It was then the middle of the winter. Roads were nearly impassable, snow was high, the jolting of the carriage threatened to shake her to pieces, but Prudence's heart was jubilant. She said to Marcia, who went with her, "No one can move events faster than the tide, but there are always those who must ride the first waves."

She returned from her trip with a roster of new students and with a deeper awareness that she had embarked on a great work. She had no fear of the future.

The new students would delight any teacher's heart, for all were bursting to learn, learn, learn. Some were daughters of well-to-do colored families. All, with one exception, were eager and able to pay the tuition. As a matter of fact, Prudence had to face earnest protests when she refused to accept the tuition on the spot. But she had made a rule that she would take no money till the student had arrived at Canterbury and begun her studies. The only exception was a girl from a poor family who was so eager for an education that a neighbor offered to pay all her expenses and required a receipt then and there.

"I was a slave," this neighbor said, "and bought my own freedom not many years ago. I know what education will mean to this girl."

The oldest of the students was a young schoolteacher from New York—hopelessly unprepared to teach—who offered her savings to Prudence for the chance of a year's study.

Prudence had been very careful to give no hint of her plans to the people of Canterbury. As soon as she knew that she had her full complement of new students, she made an announcement in *The Liberator*: "On the first Monday of April next, Miss Prudence Crandall's school will be opened for the reception of young Ladies and little Misses of color. . . . The terms, including board, washing and tuition are $25 per quarter, one half paid in advance."

That afternoon she told her old students, the daughters of the white businessmen of Canterbury, what she had done. "I hope we may remain friends, though we shall no longer be teacher and pupils. Each one of you will always be dear to me. Now good-by."

Not a girl moved. Prudence begged them to leave without emotion. Still no one moved. Then a girl rushed forward and flung her arms about Prudence, and others burst into tears and ran up to kiss her.

Prudence tried not to weep with them, but her struggle for control exhausted her more than had the jolting of the carriage over the winter roads.

The next evening four of the Canterbury fathers visited her. They told her that they had come directly from a meeting of town citizens who were alarmed at her plans, and protested vigorously.

She answered calmly that her plans were made, and that twenty new students would arrive by April first.

The men were appalled. They exploded into words. They loudly protested. They painted a picture of riot.

Prudence refused to be swayed by their threats.

Finally Mr. Frost caught his breath. "Have you considered the dangers of educating people beyond their station?" he demanded.

"How can we afford to educate Negroes who can never profit from it?" Dr. Harris flung at her.

She answered simply, "I have indeed considered the power of education."

It was a proud and defiant reply, and when they left the men were pale with anger. A town meeting would deal with her and she would regret her obstinacy!

Prudence must have realized how quickly Garrison's warnings had been fulfilled. Within a matter of hours the charming town had ceased to exist for her.

The call for the town meeting was inflammatory. Excitement mounted like a bonfire. Not only did the citizens of the township pour in from the outlying sections for the meeting, but visitors from other towns began to arrive as well.

Not all the visitors were enemies of Prudence. Garrison had sent some wise and experienced friends to stand with her—Arnold Buffum of Providence, George Benson of Boston, the Reverend Samuel May of nearby Brooklyn, Connecticut. When identified as friends of hers, they were roughly handled by the townsmen, but antislavery men were used to such treatment.

She begged them to speak for her since women could not speak in public. Indeed they would! was the answer. That was the reason they had come.

Buffum, a Quaker, offered her comfort. "Thee has drawn thyself more praying friends than the population of Canterbury." And George Benson assured her that the importance of her undertaking outweighed all the dangers. "Mr. Garrison says you must be sustained at all hazards, for if the enemies of this school triumph, other schools for Negroes will suffer in consequence."

The meeting was stormy. Speech after speech inflamed the townspeople against Prudence, who had remained at home. Marcia was listening outside the window of the meeting house and caught phrases now and then. "Reckless . . . property no longer safe . . . break down natural distinction between black and white . . . open door here and Connecticut will become overrun by Negroes . . . appeal to all Christians, loyal Americans!"

Buffum and May tried to speak, but they were shouted down as "foreigners." They retaliated by leaping onto their seats and shouting, "Town rights are not as important as the principles of truth and justice!" The town answered this by emptying the meeting house.

Marcia ran home to tell Prudence what she had heard. Prudence's answer was a brave one. "Perhaps we shall not teach history only but make it!"

At dinner that night Prudence and her three new friends thought the water tasted strangely. They discovered that a load of manure had been dumped into the well.

The crucial day, the day of the new students, was warm and sunny. Twelve girls arrived, some by stagecoach from New York, some by stage from Boston. Soft-spoken, quietly dressed, all were Negroes.

Every student knew what faced her. But every student and every student's parent felt that manure in the drinking water was not half as corrupting as a lack of education.

Dinner that first night was abundant but it consisted only of fish. Every shopkeeper in Canterbury had refused to sell provisions to Prudence. If her brother had not gone out and fished until he had enough for the household, they would have gone hungry. Prudence's father, who had brought a barrel of rainwater, promised eggs, flour, and milk if Prudence would keep up her courage.

There was nothing wrong with Prudence's courage. In the dead of that first night she heard eggs breaking against her windows. Unwilling to disturb or endanger Marcia or Almira, she went down all alone into the dark to wash the windows clean. This took much courage, but she was determined her new students should not see these signs of hate.

Classes were begun that morning in a warm, loving atmosphere. The rain was pouring outside; it continued to pour for several days, preventing the daily walk of students, two by two. This gave them all a breathing space and, perhaps, a false sense of peace. When the sun shone again, and her students went in a long decorous line for a walk, the horror started.

Boys ran beside the girls, jeering, throwing stones. The girls looked straight ahead, but it was difficult not to jump when a stone reached its mark or whizzed past a girl's head.

When the girls reached home they were trembling, but their ordeal was not over. They found a load of garbage, a dead cat, chicken heads and feet, piled at the front door. Without a word the little procession swerved and went around to the kitchen door.

Safe in the house, Prudence merely said her brother was coming that evening and he would bury the garbage around the lilacs to make them grow better in the spring.

From that time on there was no peace. That is, no peace outside the school. Inside, everyone was calm, composed. Classes were held, meals were cooked and eaten, jokes made. The girls were Prudence's strength. Samuel May said to her, "These young girls do not need to be challenged to put on strength so much as they need to be assured that kindness still lives in the world and that its expression has many forms."

The kindnesses were wonderful. Garrison assured her that every antislavery person in the country was giving them love, prayers, and support. When the cruelties came thick and fast, she remembered this.

Prudence's father was warned by the constable not to bring her any supplies unless he wished his daughter's house to be torn down by a mob. But Prudence's father appeared with his usual supplies.

Then the Vagrant Law was invoked against the colored girls who had no visible means of support. (Apparently the idea of Negroes spending entire days being educated was too improbable to believe.) The extreme penalty was a whipping on the bare back. When the constable came to administer the public beating, Prudence shut the door in his face and immediately sent an urgent message to Samuel May. He arrived as quickly as a horse would bring him, slipping into the house after dark.

She told him that every girl had offered to be the one to receive the lashing. Ann Eliza Hammond had been selected because of her great dignity.

May told her that since her call he had raised $10,000 and already posted a bond which canceled any charge of vagrancy.

During the night the strain, and the relief, were too much for Prudence. She became so ill that Almira ran to the doctor for help. The door was slammed in her face. The doctor had been told not to give aid to anyone at the school.

Prudence's enemies were gathering strength. Under

their pressure—led by Andrew Judson—the state legislature hurriedly passed a law denying the right of anyone
to set up a school for colored students unless the town
agreed.

The day after the law was passed Prudence conducted
her classes as usual and thus became a bona fide law-
breaker.

She was arrested.

The constable said she would not need her bag. She
answered that it carried neither firearms nor arrows, but
merely a few feminine articles which if displayed openly
might embarrass him.

She was brought before the judges of the local court
who assumed that she would post a bond.

"I am prepared to receive the full penalty of the law,"
said Prudence.

This was not at all what they wanted. "Perhaps you
do not understand, Miss Crandall. There is no need a
all for you to go to jail if your friends are willing to post
bonds."

"My school has many patrons," she replied. "I myself
have many supporters. May I ask you to proceed with
your duty."

They knew and she knew that nothing would point
up the outrageous situation so effectively as a woman like
her going to jail.

The jail doors closed after her.

She was released the next day, but the mere fact of her
imprisonment accomplished more for her cause than a
million words of protest.

Three of the ablest lawyers in the North volunteered
to defend her. Letters of support poured in. Arthur Tap-
pen, a millionaire antislavery man offered unlimited funds.

People who had paid little attention to the grievous problems of northern Negroes were now wakened out of their sleep.

Her trial took place in August. Her accusers tried to keep the proceedings as inconspicuous as possible. The newspapers of Connecticut had agreed not to print a word. But Prudence smiled when she saw two men in the court writing furiously. These two men represented a newssheet established for the express purpose of carrying news of her trial farther and wider than her enemies could ever reach.

The trial became narrowed to a simple proposition: No state could withhold education from any citizen. *But* Negroes, freed or enslaved, could not become citizens.

Prudence's lawyers contended that the "black laws" which prohibited citizenship to Negroes were unconstitutional.

Since this was a criminal case, the jury had to decide both law and fact. The jury could not reach agreement.

Twice the judge told them to return to the jury room and bring in a verdict. At last the foreman said that seven were for conviction, five for acquittal—and there they stood!

The judge ordered Prudence held in bail for another trial in December.

Her friends crowded around to congratulate her. With her friends was a man she did not know. He was pleasant and attractive in appearance, not an antislavery man but enormously impressed by the whole occasion. His name was Calvin Philleo. He was a minister on his way to a new church in Ithaca, New York. He asked to drive her home.

When they parted later in the day she promised to write him.

From that time on, her enemies flung all their power against her. A new and dreadful kind of persecution followed. Efforts were made to get her students to testify against her. Scarcely a day went by that a new state attorney did not appear with some fresh legal authority to compel this testimony.

The girls steadfastly refused to speak in any way. Even a defense of Prudence might be twisted against her, as they knew. One girl was jailed for her refusal. A friend of Prudence's, the Reverend Kneeland, was also jailed for declining to answer questions.

An effort was made to arrest Almira, but not even a venal judge would sustain such a writ.

Meanwhile Prudence was standing before the anti-slavery world like a light on a high hill. More influential visitors came to her school than she would have dreamed possible. Her students competed with each other to show how much they had learned. One recited a poem she had written, beginning "But we forgive, forgive the men!" and concluding on a heavenly strain:

> Where all the just surround the throne,
>   Both white and sable too,
> And there partake the feast prepared
>   For Gentile and for Jew.

Opinion was beginning to turn in her favor—little eddies, but enough to worry her prosecutors. Her second trial was abruptly called two months before it was scheduled. Prudence's courage nearly failed her when she learned that her judge was to be a man notorious for his anti-Negro views.

Her friends, caught unawares, could not be with her. She needed some tangible symbol to give her courage. On the mantel was a stone which had been thrown through the window and which she had kept as a momento. It was the size of a small cabbage—also the size of a foundation stone!

"I shall carry it in my reticule if I must," she said to her sister, smiling.

"They will think thee is carrying ammunition," Almira replied.

"So I shall be, for my conscience," Prudence answered, stroking the stone. "Mark my words, sister, if the day comes when I cannot forgive the wrongs done to me, I shall give up the school."

The second trial was an uproar. Prudence was judged guilty. Her lawyers would, of course, appeal and carry her case to the state supreme court. She was released on bail.

For the first time Prudence wondered if she would have the strength to live through the next eleven months of uncertainty.

Her attorney understood her dismay. He said, "As we gain time, your defense grows."

She saw how right he was, for she received letters from as far away as Scotland and England pledging support. The school was crammed now with students. The greater the danger, the more Negro girls offered themselves to the school. A Negro man, Mr. Olney, came from as far as Norwich to repair a clock and refused to accept any pay. He offered to help in other ways, and returned often.

During those difficult months Prudence and Calvin Philleo had corresponded regularly. Prudence had come to depend on the support and encouragement his letters offered, looking forward eagerly to their arrival. Friendship developed into love. Now Calvin asked her to marry him and she accepted.

They made no elaborate wedding plans, however, for

most of Prudence's time and energy were devoted to maintaining her school in the face of growing opposition. The people of Canterbury seemed obsessed. Returning home one evening, Prudence thought she smelled smoke. Nothing could be found. Next morning, however, Marcia saw flames under the steps. Paper shavings and small dried sticks, tucked well out of sight, had at last set fire to the decayed wood of the steps.

Prudence and the girls put out the fire. That evening a delegation from the town arrived.

"We are agitated in the extreme, Miss Crandall, to know that your house and the entire town of Canterbury so nearly escaped being reduced to ashes."

Prudence thanked them, saying it gave her some comfort to receive their apology.

Apology? That was not why they had come. They had come to formally charge her with having set the fire!

"You are tired of your school and would like to be rid of it, but your accomplice was not skilled enough in arson to succeed. He has been arrested."

She was appalled. Who arrested?

"The man last seen working in your house, a certain Olney from Norwich."

Prudence sent for Samuel May. In tears she said that indignities and inconvenience were one thing, but to endanger the lives of her students and to arrest innocent friends was another.

"You cannot abandon the school now. I beg you to hold on!"

She knew she had to hold on but wondered how much longer she could. When her friend Mr. Olney was released, she felt a great burden lifted.

Her appeal was heard that fall. It was based on the constitutionality of citizenship for free Negroes. The legal status of free Negroes was becoming such a delicate issue in every northern state that the decision in Prudence's appeal was awaited breathlessly.

The judges knew this. They declined to rule, making the excuse of a technicality in the brief.

This lack of courage on the judges' part exposed Prudence to the furious anger of Canterbury. Samuel May devoutly hoped the townspeople would not take the law into their own hands. "I would feel better, Prudence," he commented, "if during the weeks to come you had a man in the house."

Prudence smiled, a little ironically perhaps. "Samuel, this household of women has proved able to withstand the attacks of the men of the town."

But Samuel's wish was granted. That very day a man appeared—Calvin Philleo came to claim his bride.

Two weeks later the students were given an unexpected holiday in the middle of the week. That evening Prudence introduced her husband to the girls of her school.

This handsome, impressive man seemed to quiet Prudence's enemies. A few weeks of calm gave everyone hope. Then one night the household was wakened by the mysterious eerie tolling of the church bell. The bell had hardly become silent before a terrible crash came at the window.

It was like a nightmare. The whole house shook as clapboards were torn from the walls, sashes ripped from the windows, every pane of glass shattered. The assault was so massive that in a few moments the outside of the house was a wreck.

Without a word Calvin and Marcia started to sweep up the broken glass from the floors. They dared not light candles or lamps. In the dark Calvin heard the hysterical sobbing of his wife. "I hate them—I hate them!"

"Then," he said, "you must close the school. You are helpless if you hate them."

He knew that it was not hate alone but also exhaustion. Prudence was at the end of her endurance. He took her in his arms and tried to make her understand that even the enforced closing of the school could become a victory. For it would compel people everywhere to face the issues.

To Prudence who had hoped so much, such a decision seemed almost unbearable. Samuel May who was asked to explain the closing of the school to the girls was even more bitter.

"I am ashamed of Canterbury. I am ashamed of Connecticut, ashamed of my country, ashamed of my color."

The girls wept, Prudence wept with them. It seemed like defeat. Calvin, however, had prophesied more correctly than he knew.

Prudence Crandall's name became inseparable from Negro education in the North. Schools for Negroes began to burgeon.

Within five years Prudence's greatest enemy, Andrew Judson, was defeated for Congress. At the same time the Connecticut Legislature repealed the "black laws" which had put such a terrible burden on the Negroes of the state.

Prudence and Calvin opened another school in Illinois which flourished. As the whole issue of freedom and slavery deepened, Prudence's name became one of the most honored in Connecticut.

THREE

Elizabeth
Cady Stanton

U NTIL early in the twentieth century the rights of an unmarried woman were invested in her father or her brother. The rights of a married woman were summed up very simply: A husband and wife are one and that "one" is the husband.

Dorothea Dix and Prudence Crandall had found it necessary to ask men to act as their spokesmen if they wished to accomplish anything. Elizabeth Cady Stanton spent most of her life fighting for the right of a woman to function as an independent human being.

Nowadays we take for granted woman's right to hold property, sign papers, spend her own salary, have control of her children equal to her husband's, vote in elections, dispose of her time as she sees fit. But every one of these rights is very recent and has been gained only as the result of deep humiliation to women and bitter legal and legislative battles.

Elizabeth Cady was born in 1815 in Johnstown, New York. Her father was a succesful lawyer and a newly elected congressman. He was very fond of his family of five girls and one son, and was determined that they were all to have equally good educations, that is, as far as early schooling went. His son would naturally go to the university and into a profession.

Elizabeth's desire for knowledge was merely stimulated, not satisfied, by the "good" education. If her father had not allowed her to sit in his law office and listen to his talk with clients and other lawyers, she would have exploded with the frustrations of her inquiring mind.

She asked and asked and asked, and by much asking found answers to many questions. What she could *do* with the answers was another matter.

When she was eleven, her brother was killed. This nearly broke her father's heart. Elizabeth, who loved her father dearly, tried to give him some comfort, but all he could do was moan and say, "Oh, my daughter, I wish that you were a son."

Elizabeth tried to fulfil that wish. She persuaded the Presbyterian minister to teach her Greek. She fought hard to be taught Latin and higher mathematics. She was a good student in all subjects, but she found that none of this impressed her father. She was still a girl, still unable to be a lawyer or bring credit or distinction to the family as a son could do.

Even if she became a teacher, she would never gain any academic fame, for a girl could not enroll in universities and acquire degrees: she would always be obliged to teach at a primary level, at half the wages of a man.

The only "right" she had was to marry and merge her identity with her husband's.

It took Elizabeth a long time to accept these facts. At fifteen she tried to be accepted at Union College, where her brother had been a student, and the refusal, so flat and final, aroused all her rebellion. The best her father could do was send her to the Academy at Troy, New York, recently opened by Emma Willard. The Academy was considered quite revolutionary in the courses it offered to girls. Its existence, however, only served to stress the fact that women were not permitted the advantages of higher education.

Elizabeth was extremely pretty, gay, and friendly. Many

of her classmates were girls of lively minds, curious and interested in the world around them. Elizabeth had discussions and arguments with them and with their brothers, becoming increasingly aware of the need for change in the world in which they all lived.

These discussions sharpened her wits. The arguments turned more and more often to the rights of women, and many of the boys teased her with the fact that when she married she would not own anything, not even her clothes. Everything would belong to her husband.

Marriage! Elizabeth did not want it if it meant that she herself would cease to exist. Her bewilderments were deep. In those days, the traditional ways of thinking and old legalisms were beginning to be challenged, but very tentatively and slowly. The stagnant air was being stirred. However well-bred people, like the Cadys, wished no part in the change.

Intellectually Judge Cady might know that slavery was a wicked thing, but the law protected it and he was there to enforce the law. Though the indigent insane might be hideously treated, it was better to say nothing than to stir up doubts of law and order. Though homeless children, the sick, the alcoholic, the poor, might appeal to his compassion, he, as a mainstay of the law, refused to agitate the forces of rebellion which might stir up worse consequences.

Elizabeth, however, was too rebellious and young to have her father's caution. When she went to Peterborough, New York, to visit her cousin Gerrit Smith (a man much older than herself) she was suddenly confronted by a secret world which astonished and fascinated her.

Owner of a vast and rich estate, Gerrit Smith, far richer and more important than Elizabeth's father, was dedicated to the antislavery cause—dedicated, in fact, to the bitter need of having to act outside the law in order to uphold basic human rights.

In a supposedly unused wing of the Smith house a light, shining briefly, could been seen at times. This, Elizabeth discovered, signaled the arrival of a runaway slave being smuggled on to Canada and freedom . . . Elizabeth soon learned that she was visiting in a "station" of the Underground Railroad.

The people she met through her cousin were men and women of character and intelligence who were setting themselves against slavery and other social evils of the age. Their antislavery talk was rich and vivid. Elizabeth listened to their description of a riot in Philadelphia during which Pennsylvania Hall had been burned down because of an antislavery meeting held in it. And to her delight she learned that women had taken part in the meeting, had spoken from the platform as freely as men, and had shown no fear when the riot began.

She hardly knew what to think. But she knew she felt alive and eager to delve more deeply into this changing world.

One day her cousin came to her and asked her to go with him, saying that he had an important secret to share. She followed him with pounding heart, suspecting that this would be a crucial moment in her life. As he led her down an unfamiliar corridor, he made her promise that she would keep the secret for at least twenty-four hours.

When he threw open a door and stood aside, Elizabeth saw a beautiful girl, pale-skinned, black-haired, extremely nervous. Gerrit Smith said to the girl, "Harriet, my dear, I want you to tell your story with your own lips." He then left the two girls together, knowing that the story would be best told with no man about.

The girl's voice was so low that Elizabeth could hardly

hear her, but the story she unfolded chilled Elizabeth's heart.

Harriet had only one-eighth Negro blood, but that small portion classified her as a slave. She was only eighteen, yet for four years she had been owned by one New Orleans man after another. Each had used her as a prostitute and then passed her on to a friend.

Like many slaves she knew that if she could reach the safety of an Underground Railroad "station" she would be helped on to freedom in Canada. The journey from New Orleans had been long and dangerous. A girl of her beauty and grace, dressed as well as she was, might have passed for a white lady. But since she had no money and no escort, she was exposed to every humiliation and in the end her position was far more dangerous than if she had tried to escape in disguise.

By a miracle she had finally managed to reach antislavery friends. Her new friends had passed her from one devoted helper to the next until she reached the last stage of her journey—the massive support of Gerrit Smith.

She wept as she told her story, and Elizabeth wept with her. The two girls were the same age. In one helpless Negro girl Elizabeth saw with unbearable vividness a dual enslavement, that of women and Negroes.

Gerrit Smith had wished to make his young cousin face the future with her eyes wide open. He had succeeded.

Elizabeth began to stay with her cousin more often and to learn from him. His huge estate was hospitable to many visitors. On Sundays his guests would start out, in a line of carriages, to hear first a sermon at a church and then, at some Quaker meeting house or public hall, an antislavery lecture.

The lecturers belonged to that remarkable breed of men and women, beginning to crisscross the land, who faced mobs, were pelted by fusillades of eggs and rotten fruit, but who never faltered.

One Sunday Gerrit Smith's guests started out with a special interest. The antislavery speaker that day was a young man in his early thirties who was already well known for his courage and oratorical brilliance. His record was heroic. He had faced mobs in every state from Indiana to Maine. His name was Henry Brewster Stanton.

Elizabeth listened to him enraptured. He was handsome in a strong, sturdy way. He spoke so well that he either aroused passionate admiration or passionate hate, never indifference. Elizabeth gave him passionate admiration.

Henry Stanton returned with them to Gerrit Smith's estate. The two men had many plans to discuss, many new techniques for antislavery agitation to plan with scrupulous care. Stanton and Smith believed the country was ready for startling challenges, perhaps even a political party dedicated to the end of slavery.

Gerrit Smith always included his womenfolk—his wife, his daughter and cousin and guests—in such conversations. Elizabeth found herself arguing and asking any questions that occurred to her. Young Henry Stanton was the one who replied. Elizabeth found him even more stimulating than the law students in her father's office.

Those were wonderful days. She was free and happy and part of an exhilarating world in which women had a place. When, one day, Henry took her out riding and asked her to marry him, she agreed without hesitation. She loved him.

Although both of them would be bound by the laws which made Henry master of his wife, legally and morally, Henry would do everything in his power to see that her own identity and self-respect were preserved. He wanted her to be a full individual in her own right. It was nothing short of a miracle that such a man had come into her life and that she loved him.

Gerrit Smith was delighted that this romance had developed under his roof. But as an experienced man he warned her that her father would *not* be delighted, and she could not marry without her father's consent. Henry's precarious living came in ways which would be appalling to her father.

Elizabeth protested furiously. Henry had saved three thousand dollars; what more did they need? At last she agreed to write to her father, putting the matter in the best possible light. Her father did not reply. She knew now that she would have to confront him face to face.

He was as angry as Gerrit Smith had foretold. He called Henry an adventurer who wanted only her money. She threatened to elope. He said an elopement would not be a legal marriage and that Henry would discard her when he found another woman more to his liking.

Elizabeth was reduced to helpless tears. After all, she did not know Henry very well. Although his letters were constant and loving, her father and her brother-in-law managed to throw continual doubt upon Henry's reasons for wishing to marry her. At last in despair she agreed to break the engagement.

But Henry was used to fighting for what he believed in, and Elizabeth, fortunately, had a sister, Madge, who taunted Elizabeth with being fainthearted and not true to herself.

Henry continued to write every day. Madge compelled her to read the letters. When Henry said he was leaving for England to attend an antislavery convention in London, Elizabeth went deadly white. That was all Madge needed to know. She and Elizabeth faced their father together, and the judge capitulated. He still disapproved, but he was too good a lawyer not to recognize a lost case.

There was no time for a fashionable wedding. Only just time for Henry to arrive, for Elizabeth to persuade the minister to omit the word "obey" in the marriage service, and for Elizabeth, Henry, and Madge to hurry by Hudson River boat to New York where a tall-masted ship would carry the Stantons to England.

Henry was one of the chief American delegates to the convention. William Lloyd Garrison, Wendell Phillips, James and Lucretia Mott—women were delegates, Elizabeth learned to her joy; seven of them!—were coming by another ship.

One of the delegates, traveling on the ship which carried the Stantons, was James G. Birney, a remarkable man in all ways but one.

Birney was a Southerner from Alabama who had freed his slaves, moved to Ohio, and joined the fight against slavery. But this remarkable man, who had fought an entire system with great courage, was abysmally conservative toward other forms of emancipation. For example, he believed that the Bible taught the subservient position of women, because the second chapter of Genesis said Eve was created after Adam!

Elizabeth's carefree ways, her habit of calling her husband "Henry" in public rather than "Mr. Stanton," left Birney aghast. He was not the only one shocked by her. Most of the passengers shared his views. Henry was somewhat amused when Mr. Birney took it upon himself to coach Elizabeth in the proper behavior of a delegate's wife. After all, Mr. Birney reasoned, as antislavery people they were controversial enough without a gay and inexperienced bride attracting attention.

Elizabeth took his disapproval cheerfully, learned what she could from this shrewd and pompous man, and then fled to her husband or to the ship's captain for a breath of fresh air.

The captain was certainly her friend. He provided her with a bosun's chair which he ordered hoisted to the masthead where Elizabeth could swing happily for hours, reading and studying.

London in June was beautiful. Delegates to the convention had come from many countries. Henry, writing to the New York newspapers, said antislavery "wore golden slippers in London." By this he meant that antislavery was fashionable with titled and rich English people. Neither Henry nor Elizabeth was prepared for a deep humiliation administered by their own delegation.

James G. Birney stood up and protested the presence of the seven women delegates. He protested so vigorously and with such logic that many in the gathering supported his proposal that the women be excluded from participation.

Wendell Phillips rose immediately. Wendell Phillips was one of the great antislavery figures. He protested the motion with all the vigor and power of his beautiful voice. He was experienced enough to know that a painful infection had reached a critical point. For many months conservative men in the antislavery ranks had been growing more and more afraid that the cause would be made to look "ridiculous" if women were allowed to continue as speakers or delegates.

Strong and glowing women, such as Lucretia Mott, Sarah and Angelina Grimké (rich sisters from a slaveowning South Carolina family), Abby Kelly, and Sojourner Truth were known to be even more effective speakers than the men.

Phillips now made a motion that any delegate who carried proper credentials from an antislavery society—anywhere in the world—must be admitted to the proceedings.

Pandemonium broke loose. From every part of the floor men sprang up, shouting that they had come to free slaves, not women! Men in the black clothes of clergymen were crying out hysterically that women were *born* inferior to men and must accept their God-given lot!

The women were fascinated as they listened. To most of them this was an old story. They smiled somewhat grimly at the wry compromise: the women delegates would be allowed to remain in the hall, but they must sit apart, withdraw to a screened-off section of the auditorium where they could hear but not be seen or take part in the voting.

On the day of their banishment Elizabeth walked beside Lucretia Mott back to their lodgings. Mrs. Mott was twice Elizabeth's age, a woman of beauty and distinction who had spent her adult life pleading for every underprivileged living thing in the world. Elizabeth was badly shaken by what she had heard that day, and she cried, "The time has come. Women's rights are as important as the slaves'!"

Lucretia nodded with a smile. Perhaps she had been waiting for just such a young woman. "Yes," she said. "I have been saying that for years. Now it must be said from the housetops."

But they began their campaign in the dining room with Mr. Birney. He might control the convention floor, but he was not master here. All the women, delegates and wives of delegates, bombarded him with logic. He could not contradict it. After a few days, his mealtimes ruined, he moved to another hotel.

Within the convention there were undoubtedly some very uneasy moments while they awaited the arrival of the man whose prestige was international. William Lloyd Garrison, some believed, would dissent in an even more powerful voice than Wendell Phillips had.

He arrived five days late and promptly spoke his mind. Instead of the great speech which had been eagerly anticipated by delegates, spectators, and the newspapers, he said simply and bitterly: "After battling so many long years for the liberties of the African slaves, I cannot countenance any action that strikes down the sacred rights of women *everywhere!*"

To a clatter heard round the world, he then left the platform, walked straight across the floor to the alcove to which the women had been relegated, and sat down with them.

He did not speak another word during the whole convention, and his silence was the loudest speech there.

Elizabeth really grew up during these days. Incisive, intelligent, with a sharp turn of phrase, she made a vivid impression on the other delegates. Garrison, always quick and shrewd in his evaluation of a man or a woman, paid special heed to Elizabeth. Lucretia Mott wrote home that all Henry's friends were very happy that he had a bride who was capable of being his equal.

Elizabeth herself knew how miraculous it was to have a husband like Henry. This trip was not only a honeymoon but a university course. A new world had opened up.

Dining one day with the great Daniel O'Connell, who fought brilliantly in Parliament for social and political freedoms, Elizabeth asked him many questions. He had gained much and lost much. Did he ever feel he had overreached himself?

"No," he said. "It is always good policy to claim the uttermost, for then at least you are sure to get something."

When the Stantons returned to the United States both knew they stood at a crossroads. Elizabeth had been so deeply moved by her experiences that she scarcely knew which way she wished most to turn. Yet when she was asked what had made the deepest impression on her abroad, she had answered spontaneously, "Lucretia Mott!" This was more than a hint of her future.

But certain realities had first to be faced. Elizabeth was expecting a baby. Henry, as head of a family, knew his lecturing and traveling days were over. He opened a law practice in Boston and took several unpopular cases. Elizabeth gave birth to a boy and showed some of her new principles by refusing to swaddle him and by adopting new, revolutionary methods of child care.

Eight years passed. Two more children were born. Elizabeth was caught, willy-nilly, by the demands of a family and Henry by his growing law practice. But both of them seized every chance to talk with their antislavery friends. These friends were busy in every phase of emancipation. The Married Woman's Property Bill finally passed the New York State legislature largely through their efforts. Elizabeth was proud and jubilant.

For the first time, married women were permitted to own property in their own names, not their husband's, and to collect rents and profits, and to sell. It was daring; it caused great excitement.

In 1847 the Stantons moved to Seneca Falls, New York. During the summer of 1848 Lucretia Mott came to visit a friend nearby. Elizabeth went to see her. It was a social visit, nothing more.

But these were two exceptional women. They were not content to sit about and talk idly. Elizabeth felt that the time had come to take hold of the future and give it the shape they desired.

Before the day was over, Lucretia Mott and Elizabeth decided to call a women's rights convention—the first such convention in the history of the world.

The next day in the *Seneca County Courier* startled readers were faced by a call to action:

A convention to discuss the social, civil and religious conditions and rights of women will be held in the Wesleyan Chapel at Seneca Falls, New York, on Wednesday and Thursday, the 19th and 20th of July current, commencing at 10 o'clock A.M. During the first day the meeting will be exclusively for women, which all are earnestly invited to attend. The public generally are invited to be present on the second day when Lucretia Mott of Philadelphia and others, both ladies and gentlemen, will address the convention.

They had exactly five days to prepare for "the most momentous reform that had yet been launched into the world." As Elizabeth described it: "The first organized protest against the injustice which has brooded for ages over the character and destiny of one half the race."

In the meantime Elizabeth deluged Henry with questions. She wanted legal parallels that would make their formal declaration as close to the Declaration of Independence as possible. He searched the statute books. She returned to the home of Lucretia Mott's friend, and for five days the women sat around the dining room table planning for the convention. Not one of them knew parliamentary procedure or how to conduct a meeting. Lucretia Mott frowned deeply, trying to remember temperance and antislavery convention rules. Between her recollections and their common sense they evolved a procedure.

At home Elizabeth rehearsed over and over the best gestures and voice inflections for her speech. Henry was an audience of one. He was stern and exacting. He insisted she must organize her points like a debater.

Henry loved his Elizabeth very much. He was determined that every loophole should be blocked through which any discredit to a woman might creep in. She was an attractive and persuasive speaker, and as the week went on his anxiety began to recede. All would be well.

Elizabeth also gained confidence. She gained such confidence that she resolved to add one more crucial note to her speech—a note that even Lucretia Mott was unwilling to sound.

She would ask for the right of women to vote.

Henry was aghast. Not because he disagreed—he thought women should be allowed to vote, or at least bright ones like his Elizabeth!—but because he did not believe the convention could survive the ridicule and anger that would result from such a request.

He paced up and down. He begged her to reconsider. He said if she insisted he would have to stay away, for he could not bear to witness the mockery of his "lovely Lee."

Elizabeth did not want to oppose Henry. She knew he had made their happy marriage possible by his high regard for women. But she had to tell him that, however nervous and frightened she might feel, she must carry through her demand for the vote.

Henry said nothing more. Elizabeth's apprehensions deepened. They reached a near panic when word came that Lucretia's husband, James Mott, who had agreed to be chairman of the meeting, was sick. Even Lucretia herself might not be able to attend.

Without Lucretia's maturity and experience, Elizabeth and the other women felt as helpless as children. But there was no turning back.

As Elizabeth arranged flowers on the day of the convention, her hands were shaking so badly that she could not imagine how she or the others would survive the next few hours. Men, women, and children were already arriving in buggies with picnic baskets to spend the day at the convention, and some of them had come to make trouble.

Elizabeth's relief was immense when the Motts arrived at the last moment. James was still a bit shaky, but he called the meeting promptly to order.

These two days, July 19 and 20, 1848, were among the most important days in America's history. The women of America would not receive the vote for another seventy years, but from that time onward the outcome was inevitable. This little Seneca Falls convention, organized by a handful of inexperienced women on a moment's notice, was such a trumpet call that the ignoble position of women could no longer be ignored.

Elizabeth found her full identity that first day.

She dominated the convention, not because she wanted to but because she found unexpected powers in herself. Pretty, young, intelligent, she set forth the problems that women had to meet. They were summed up in the words she used on that occasion: Men had "endeavored in every way to destroy [woman's] confidence in her own powers, to lessen her self-respect, and to make her willing to lead a dependent and abject life."

The discussion that followed justified the whole convention. Women in the audience lost their shyness and rose to speak. The legal enslavement of women—its cause, its effects—were discussed and resolutions prepared while picnic baskets rattled and children wailed.

Frederick Douglass, the great Negro abolitionist, was there, and two or three other Negro men and women underlined the inseparable nature of the two enslavements.

On the second and last day the resolutions were to be voted on. Elizabeth was determined to offer her resolution on voting, although Lucretia Mott still shook her head . . . too fast, too soon. Elizabeth was desperately unhappy. Her path looked a very lonely one. But Frederick Douglass spoke up suddenly. He said she was absolutely right. Negroes and women, he insisted, could accomplish nothing without the vote. As it stood, neither was a citizen.

Blushing and almost in tears, she offered her resolution. Her voice must have sounded very small. But as the reaction broke over her head, she gained confidence and eloquence.

She defended her resolution well and vividly. Douglass rose and used his formidable eloquence in her support. When the voting came the resolution was passed—by the narrowest possible margin, it is true, but it passed— and wrecked the convention. Thus Henry's fears were justified—all but his worst fear. His "lovely Lee" had emerged as a woman of whom he was proud. She might suffer, she might be reviled, but her intelligence and her power had been tested and found true.

Elizabeth needed Henry's support more than ever—all the women who had stood steadfast needed reassurance— for the little convention hidden away in a small town had wide repercussions. The dissenters had carried their outrage to the public and Elizabeth, Lucretia, and the others were dumfounded to learn that not only American newspapers but also European were blazoning the story in scandalized tones. "The most shocking and unnatural incident ever recorded in the history of womaninity . . ." began the *Oneida Whig*. PETTICOATS VS. BOOTS headlined another newspaper. Ministers denounced the convention from their pulpits.

This was hard on many of the women who had made

up the audience at Seneca Falls. With scandal threatening, they asked to have their names removed from the declaration. Elizabeth saw women with whom she had been friendly for many years cross the street rather than speak to her. From Johnstown came the thunder of her father's wrath, threatening to disinherit her. But Elizabeth was aware of something even more remarkable. She was aware that the tide was beginning to turn.

Within the year, women in Ohio, Pennsylvania, Indiana, Massachusetts—and twice again in New York State—gathered in conventions and the world was forced to listen.

Lacking precedents for their suffragist activities, each step Elizabeth and others like her took was fresh and raw and trail-blazing. Not only must she and the other women learn how to live and work in public—and in the midst of a hostility that amounted to fury—but they must learn to be even better wives and mothers.

Elizabeth had four children now. Whenever she spoke in public someone was bound to charge her with being unnatural, unwomanly, neglectful of helpless and innocent children. But she was prepared. When rich and fashionable mothers went to Saratoga or Newport, they left their children at home, "but my children are right here in town with me, in charge of a nurse. And when I have finished we will all go home together."

Her reputation as a speaker was growing. Many women began to feel that she was a better advocate of their cause than the men who had appeared for them. Dr. William Ellery Channing, Dorothea Dix's great friend, said that no man he knew presented his points as arrestingly or with as much personal charm as she did. Perhaps only Henry knew how she suffered from shyness and what endless courage it took for her to get up on a platform.

Henry was subject to even more abuse than she. He was

running for state senator on the Free Soil ticket and had to defend his wife as well as himself in his speeches. But he won. This, perhaps more than anything else, showed that the change in the times ran deeper than most people were willing to admit.

A Woman's Rights' Conference was called for Albany, New York, in 1854. The women decided to make a strong stand for new legislation. Elizabeth was selected to represent them, to speak in that formidable legislative chamber, facing row upon row of lawmakers (if they would attend, that is!). Most of the men would be ruthlessly critical, not so much because she was a woman but because legal matters were being discussed of which she, in all modesty, should know nothing.

Elizabeth had already met a remarkable woman, soon to be her closest friend and colleague, Susan B. Anthony. Susan urged her to have courage. Henry promised to assist her in every way he knew how. Elizabeth set to work to prepare her speech with more care than she had ever before prepared anything. She longed for her father's legal advice, but she dared not even tell him that she was going to Albany.

But friends and enemies hurried to tell him, and Elizabeth received a stern letter ordering her to stop at his home on her way to the capital. Her heart quailed. She knew he would do everything within his power to prevent her going on.

When she stood face to face with him in his study, he told her coldly that she would embarrass him seriously in Albany. Her failure would strike at him and him alone and he was too well known in the state capital to take this risk.

She shook her head, unable to speak. He lost his temper

and repeated what she already knew—that he had dis-
inherited her.

She found her voice then, and told him quietly that *he*
was to blame. He had raised her to listen to her conscience.
He was the first human being to point out to her the terrible inequalities of women before the law. She was exactly what he had made her.

He stared at her for some time. When he spoke, he said
unexpectedly, "Read me your speech."

Elizabeth tried to keep her hands from shaking. The
legislative body in Albany would be child's play compared
to facing her father. She closed her eyes and tried to control her voice. All her heart and spirit went into her words.

The speech was built on case after case of cruelty and
injustice: a widow thrust out of her home hours after
her husband's death, a mother unable to save her son from
being apprenticed to a gambler, another mother legally
unable to protect her daughter from being forced into a
brothel, women forcibly separated from their children for
no reason save a husband's anger.

> The wife who inherits no property holds about the same
> legal position as does the slave on the southern plantation.
> She can own nothing and sell nothing. She has no rights
> even to the wages she earns. Her person, her time, her
> services, are the property of another. Would to God you
> could know the burning indignation that fills a woman's
> soul when she sees how like feudal barons you free men
> hold your women. . . . We ask for all you have asked for
> yourselves since the *Mayflower* cast anchor beside Plymouth
> Rock, and simply on the ground that the rights of every
> human being are the same and identical.

Her father was silent for some time. Then he asked her
in a muffled voice, "How have I failed you? How has
Henry?"

She answered in surprise, "Neither you nor Henry have failed me. You have taught me to think."

Her father was silent once more. Then he said in a changed voice, in his lawyer's voice, that they must close up a few loopholes in her presentation.

Elizabeth's heart swelled with joy as he went over the speech with the eyes of a very shrewd lawyer and found the exact statute to cover every case she had raised.

When she rose in the Assembly to speak, the chamber was packed. Probably most of the lawmakers had come out of unsympathetic curiosity, but they found that this woman was as attractive and feminine as their wives, that her speech was cogent and powerful. In fact, both she and her speech were a triumph. Applause thundered when she sat down.

Her words were promptly printed by the thousands and distributed widely. Many thousands signed the petitions that the women circulated throughout the state.

But the lawmakers, for all their gallantry, talked of everything but legislation to protect women. And the newspapers continued to refer to Punch-and-Judy shows and to hens that crowed like roosters.

Elizabeth—and now Susan Anthony, who had finally agreed that women *should* have the vote—put more faith in the logic of events than in lawmakers. Words and thoughts had been set in motion, the humiliations of women, the injustices, had been brought into the open. There was nothing abstract about them. Almost every woman could cite instances of indignities. Sooner or later the inexorable force of logic would work in their behalf.

The responsibilities of husband, children, and home-making did not stop Elizabeth's public activities, but she *was* growing very tired. Susan was indispensable. Over and over Susan substituted for Elizabeth at conventions and meetings, her own shyness lessening as Elizabeth coached her carefully in facts and in procedures.

Henry said humorously, "You stir up Susan, and Susan stirs up the world!"

These two women were a remarkable team. Susan was strong on facts and figures, Elizabeth on heart and spirit. More and more women were joining their ranks—Lucy Stone, for example, whose mother had grieved at her birth because "life is so hard for a woman." Although Lucy had managed to get a degree at Oberlin, a pioneer college in Ohio, she had not been allowed to read her own essay at commencement. She had indignantly refused the alternative offered her—to allow a male professor to read it for her—and so she had graduated in secret, as it were.

When Elizabeth was again asked to address the New York legislature in 1860, she had a sudden feeling of hope. She spoke powerfully for the bill which would allow married women to collect wages independent of their husbands, have joint guardianship of their children and, if widowed, not be dispossessed of property.

It was a history-making bill. It was passed the day after Elizabeth spoke.

It gave to women everything they had asked except the vote.

But Elizabeth, Susan, and many other civil rights women were not completely satisfied. Without a vote, women would remain in a subservient position.

In the year 1860 every hope and plan was overshadowed by the approaching Civil War. When the war began, Elizabeth and Susan found themselves lonely voices pleading that the rights of women must not be lost in the confusion of the times. They were right in their fears, for within a year the New York legislature repealed several measures supporting women's rights.

Many of the antislavery people felt that this war must be fought for the Negro exclusively, confident that women would gain as a consequence. But as the war came to an end, Susan and Elizabeth managed to get a convention together in Brooklyn and went on record as saying, "There can never be a true peace in this Republic until the civil and political rights of all citizens of African descent, and *all women*, are practically established."

They set out to try to get one million signatures on a petition stating this belief.

The extraordinary part is that the signatures poured in. But, in a way, they represented just so much paper. Even antislavery men who had stood with them so staunchly began to talk about full citizenship for the Negro as something which must be separated from women's rights.

Facts were facts, they said. The end of slavery had come in blood and tears. Now the amendments necessary to insure the Negro's actual freedom had to be fought through the halls of Congress. Even devoted friends like Wendell Phillips said, "Let the women wait." And the Republican party, which had made many vague promises to women, now said that "suffrage for the black man will be all the strain the party can stand."

This was a shock to Elizabeth and Susan. Out of this shock they made mistakes of policy which separated them from some of their friends. When they called the first Woman Suffrage Convention in Washington to agitate for a Sixteenth Amendment giving all women over twenty-one the right to vote, Congress ignored them completely, and the National Woman Suffrage Association itself split in half.

All the exhilaration and expectation of the past seemed to vanish overnight. This ironic split, when unity was so badly needed to get things going again, shook Elizabeth and Susan as nothing else had done.

They were middle-aged women, and they felt it. They had spent their whole adult lives fighting for a cause which had seemed almost in their hands. Now they had to start completely afresh.

They had to start uphill, to argue old points which everyone had heard a hundred times. With the end of the war, the country was eager to forget old sins and begin to make money. The women were told to forget everything and get back into the kitchen.

To Elizabeth's astonishment, in that same year she was asked by a lecture bureau to go on a speaking tour across the country. She could hardly believe her ears. There was money in her oft-told story? She accepted with alacrity, for no commercial lecture bureau would offer so grand a tour unless they felt this subject met popular demand.

Her seven children were grown, or old enough to manage at home. Henry promised to hold the domestic fort and kissed her good-by. Elizabeth, now plump, her curly hair white, felt like a young girl again.

The tour was an immense success. Her vivid way of expressing thoughts, her fresh charm, captivated audiences everywhere. She wrote Henry and Susan that once again the tide seemed to have turned in their favor.

She was right. In 1869 the territorial government of Wyoming gave women the right to vote. A straw in the wind, but bricks were made with straw!

For the next twelve years she went out from June to October on her lecture tours. These were lonely, tired years when she was often stuck at some crossroads town in the Wild West without transportation; but all the time she was building, slowly but surely building, opinion.

She was becoming one of the best known and best liked women in the country.

Younger women were showing a natural, eager enthusiasm for equality before the law. More and more men were defying conservatism and supporting women's rights.

Colorado was the first state to give women the vote. (New Zealand was the first country.) By 1888 women from all over the world were beginning to respond in active ways. England, France, Norway—even India—sent women to a conference in Washington that year.

Elizabeth spoke words as glowing and timeless as herself.

The promised land lay in front of them. Go in and claim it! "We are filled with wonder as to what the future mothers of the race will be."

One day, when she was eighty-seven years old, she was writing a letter to President Theodore Roosevelt. In it she urged that he be the President who had the glory of throwing wide the door for women. She died as she was writing it.

It was not until eighteen years later, when the Nineteenth Amendment was passed, that this door was opened in the United States.

When women became citizens the world was not magically changed. But is there anyone now in the world who can honestly deny the fact that all adult human beings must be responsible for their own welfare? that if things are bad it is up to them, by the power of the franchise, to make them better? that every man and woman has the right to be a full member of the family of man?

Great women—and great men—have made us see that we are all citizens of a common destiny.

FOUR

Elizabeth
Blackwell

WHILE Elizabeth Cady Stanton was trying to gain the elemental rights of citizenship for women, Elizabeth Blackwell was striving for other specific rights. She wanted the opportunity to care for the ill— to be a doctor.

She might as well have asked permission to grow two heads. A host of misconceptions rose up like barriers, impeding her efforts at every turn. Most people were convinced that it was improper for a woman to have intimate knowledge of the human body. Their arguments were as numerous as they were unreasonable: women were incapable of scientific exactness; the atmosphere of a medical school would be intolerable to a woman; no one would trust a woman doctor.

But Elizabeth Blackwell was as stubborn as Prudence Crandall or Dorothea Dix or Elizabeth Cady Stanton. She also had the advantage of a remarkable family who took for granted the equality of daughters and sons.

Her father was an Englishman, in the sugar refinery business, in Bristol, England. There Elizabeth was born in 1821. Her father had insisted that his daughters be given the same educational opportunities as his sons. He had taught them to hate slavery of every kind—the enslavement of the Negro, the enslavement of poverty, ignorance, prejudice.

When Elizabeth was eleven years old, her father's business was caught in a general business slump. From great prosperity he was suddenly struggling with disaster. He decided that in spite of its acceptance of slavery, the United States was the land of opportunity. Acting promptly, he booked passage to New York for his wife, his four sisters, and his three daughters and two sons.

Mr. Blackwell was an astute business man and he promptly established business contacts with Quakers. New York was a tumultuous city that year. Riots against the new Antislavery Society shook the streets. The Blackwells' response to this violence was to seek out all the knowledge and understanding they could of the issues involved. As a consequence, Mr. Blackwell and his family met William Lloyd Garrison, attended meetings in New York supporting Prudence Crandall's school, and participated with enthusiasm in the growing struggle for human rights.

The next five years were difficult ones for the Blackwell family. Their strong convictions and sense of justice guided their actions against entrenched public opinion. Emancipation—of women, Negroes, the sick, the poor —engrossed all the brothers and sisters.

The depression of 1837 made the family turn toward the West. Cincinnati, Ohio, was a western city in those days promising unlimited opportunities. The Blackwells arrived, lock, stock and barrel. Two years later Mr. Blackwell died suddenly, leaving only twenty-five dollars to his wife and children.

Elizabeth was then sixteen, the oldest child still living at home. She had to become the immediate support of her mother and the younger children. Opening a school or becoming a governess were the only possibilities for a respectable young lady.

With the help of a friend of her father's, Elizabeth

established a school and for six years devoted her time and energy to her pupils. The school prospered but its limitations were often frustrating and discouraging to her. Most of her students' parents did not want their children exposed to the challenging ideas that absorbed Elizabeth.

Occasionally she talked about a wider, bigger world with her two closest friends in Cincinnati—Harriet Beecher Stowe and Harriet's sister, Catherine. Catherine was already engrossed in her great dream—an educational system that would engage all of one's faculties; but Harriet's shyness at that time made it hard to foresee that she would become one of the most famous women in America.

Elizabeth was a small, slender girl, with dark hair and dark eyes, who looked as though she should be protected from the world. Far from seeking a sheltered life, however, Elizabeth was devoured by a restless eagerness to be of real use in the world. But all doors seemed closed to her and the restrictions imposed by society were compounded by her own uncertainty as to the direction of her goals.

One day she went to see a woman friend who was dying. As they talked the dying woman asked why Elizabeth did not become a doctor and try to find new ways of fighting disease.

Elizabeth had not in her wildest moments imagined such a profession. As a matter of fact, the human body and its functions had always repelled her. But she loved her friend, and the thought grew upon her of what she might have done to help had she the skill.

She spoke her thoughts aloud to Harriet Stowe, but Harriet's husband answered, "Unthinkable!"

Elizabeth, raised to consider anything possible, felt a

flare of anger. A vague plan grew into determination. She talked to her family about the matter. Her brothers were keenly excited by the idea. She went to see a friendly doctor. He told her that no true lady would be able to stand the sights and smells—and jokes—of a medical school.

Elizabeth responded to this as she had to the cry "Unthinkable!" She sent letters of inquiry to all the doctors she knew. All of them, with one exception, replied that the idea was not even to be considered for a decent Christian girl. The one exception sent her a list of medical schools.

Elizabeth was now fully roused. She—small, slight, shy —was willing to tackle the whole world if necessary to get a doctor's training. If women could not take part in the fight against pain and sickness, then women were being denied one of their truest rights.

She knew she had to have money and she had to have access to a medical library. This meant closing her school and leaving home. She was terrified of doing both. But when she learned that she could have a position as music teacher in a school run by a man who had once been a doctor, she moved swiftly. The school was in North Carolina. Her brothers offered to drive her there in the family carriage.

All the way they tried to cheer her with their enthusiasm and confidence. But during the ten-day journey Elizabeth was sick with nervousness. If the world thought she was out of her mind—well, perhaps she was. She arrived at the Dicksons' home ill and exhausted and went straight to bed.

Her brothers promised to return the next morning.

That night as she lay in a strange room, she knew that she must admit defeat—or win. "Suddenly, an answer came," she wrote later.

A brilliant light of hope and peace filled my soul. At once, I know not how, the terror fled away, my joy came back. A deep conviction came to me that my life was accepted by God, that I should be helped and guided. A peace, as to the righteousness of my course, settled down upon my mind that was never afterward destroyed. During the years that followed I suffered many bitter sorrows but I have never since been able to doubt . . . My whole temperament had been strongly susceptible to visions, or mystical influences, but this unusual experience at the outset of my medical career has had a lasting and marked effect on my whole life. To me it was a revealed experience of Truth, a direct vision of the great reality of spiritual existence, as irresistible as it is incommunicable. I shall be grateful to the last day of my life for this great gift of faith.

She had come to a family who liked and helped her. The Dicksons were friendly, music-loving people. In the evenings they played and sang. Elizabeth loved this, but she loved even more the medical books that Mr. Dickson owned. She pored over them every spare moment of the day. She was a good student and she was hungry for this knowledge. Presently her notebook and her head were crammed.

The only shadow for Elizabeth came from the slavery all about her. In the North, the idea of slavery appalled but remained out of sight. Here she saw it in all its horror. She decided to start a Sunday school for Negro children, and she gained the unexpected support of one white man and four white women, wives of slaveowners. But the law against teaching slaves harried her at every step and forced her to retreat.

It was not long before Elizabeth had exhausted the limited medical library at her disposal. Mr. Dickson suggested that she go to stay with his brother, a doctor, in Charleston, South Carolina. There she could continue her studies and support herself by giving occasional music lessons.

North Carolina had been liberal in contrast to South Carolina. The rice and cotton plantations of South Carolina encouraged the grossest mistreatment of the Negroes. Elizabeth found it almost unbearable. Even though Dr. Dickson had a splendid medical library and was kindness itself, Elizabeth felt she had to escape as soon as possible.

She saved every penny she could put her hands on and wrote letters to dozens of doctors and medical schools in the North. She received only one reply.

Dr. Joseph Warrington of Philadelphia, which was then the medical capital of the United States, did not laugh at her or ignore her, but he wrote that, in his opinion, men were intended to be doctors and women nurses. He added that several women had told him that *they* would never go to a woman doctor.

It could hardly be called an "encouraging" letter, but Elizabeth left promptly for Philadelphia. In Philadelphia were four medical schools. She asked for interviews. When she received no answers, she wrote again more insistently. A few professors agreed to talk with her. One or two said they would put her case before their colleagues. The majority refused to help in any way.

Finally, through sheer determination, she reached Dr. Warrington. He listened courteously and said her faith in herself was impressive. "Go to Paris. Disguise yourself in men's clothes and attend some of the medical lectures. One or two other women have done this with some satisfaction to themselves, but with no diploma, of course."

The suggestion made Elizabeth furious. She was willing to go anywhere, she told him, even to hell; but she would go as herself.

At length a small break came in the solid opposition. Dr. Joseph Allen, who directed the Philadelphia School of Anatomy, listened to her and said, "Do you understand what these studies will mean? You may find them too objectionable to endure."

Elizabeth said she was perfectly aware that the human body shocked some people, but she was not one of them. Her only feeling would be gratitude for the chance to learn more. Dr. Allen told her to be on hand at eight o'clock the next morning with the proper instruments.

The other students, all young men, showed a moment's amazement at seeing her, but Elizabeth's attitude, and Professor Allen's, were so objective that the young men accepted her in the best scientific spirit.

The first half-hour of the demonstration was a shock to Elizabeth. Dr. Allen laid a human arm on the long wooden table and Elizabeth had to swallow hard. But presently she lost her dismay as the doctor laid bare the amazing intricacies of muscles, nerves, and tendons. Her pencil flew over the pages of her notebook, and when the lecture was over she could hardly wait for the next day.

The course was a short one and almost immediately Elizabeth began bombarding medical schools in New York, Vermont, and the medical faculties at Harvard, Yale, and Bowdoin. In all cases "no" was the answer. Dr. Warrington then showed his liberal spirit by writing to a dozen medical schools so new they scarcely had a faculty. Only the Medical College of Geneva, New York, replied.

A letter from the dean said a resolution had been unanimously adopted: "That one of the radical principles of a Republican government is the universal education of both sexes . . . that the door should be opened equally to all . . . that in extending our unanimous invitation to Elizabeth Blackwell, we pledge ourselves that [she shall never] regret her attendance at this institution."

Elizabeth could hardly believe her eyes. Dr. Warrington was gratified and amazed. Elizabeth danced with excitment. She made immediate preparations. She traveled all night and reached Geneva the next day at midnight in a cold November rain.

She had no way of knowing that the invitation was a great joke.

She did not know that when Dr. Warrington's letter came, the dean, not wishing to offend so great a man, had told the students they would have to decide. The dean had chuckled and washed his hands of the matter, for he knew his students. They were notorious in the town for noisiness, brutality, rudeness.

They received the application "of a lady medical student" with shouts of laughter. They made hilarious speeches of mock chivalry and voted with wild abandon to admit her. The one student who voted seriously against her was wrestled to the floor and threatened with dire punishment if he did not make the vote unanimous.

The joke was, to them and to the dean, so wild and foolish that they forgot it almost immediately. Their consternation was great indeed when—on that history-making November morning—the door opened on the usual class bedlam and a small, slim, pretty girl entered shyly.

She had obviously come to stay.

A stricken silence descended. The silence continued as each young man groped for a seat and stared at this apparition. For the first time in the history of the school, a professor was able to carry his lecture through to its conclusion.

"This sudden transformation of the class from a band

of lawless desperadoes to gentlemen proved to be perma-
nent," wrote one of the "lawless desperadoes" years later
when he became Commissioner for Health in New York
City.

The "desperadoes" had a sense of fair play. They admired her refusal to be embarrassed or put off. After a
short period of confused adjustment, 150 men and one girl
settled down to serious studies.

Some of the professors were distracted by her presence, but Dr. Webster, the professor of anatomy, greeted
his first woman student with enthusiasm and foretold
a great future.

Only the townspeople would not yield in any way.
Elizabeth had great trouble finding a place to live. No one
wished to believe that a young woman who attended
that wild and indecent college could be respectable. The
room she finally found was tiny and bitterly cold. None
of her fellow boarders would speak to her. Women, meeting her on the street, drew their skirts aside as she
passed.

"I never took walks," Elizabeth wrote to a friend, "but
hurried daily to my college as a sure refuge. I knew that
when I shut the door I shut out all unkindly criticism."

But even this hostility worked itself into a small asset
for the college. Ladies of Geneva began to apply for visitors' tickets to some of the lectures in order to inspect this
dreadful young woman. But their presence, for whatever
reason, improved the classes, and the dean was soon
jubilant.

"You are a good advertisement," he told Elizabeth. "I
shall bring the matter into the medical journals. I venture
to say that in ten years' time one third of the classes in
medical colleges will consist of women."

Elizabeth's great strength lay in her determination to

maintain an attitude of scientific inquiry. She was well aware that a great many bawdy jokes were normally exchanged between professors and students. She knew that when she was in the class, the professors chose their words painstakingly. It was not an easy position for her to be in, and she had to maintain it all alone.

When her friend, the professor of anatomy, wrote her a kindly but awkward letter saying that he would find it very difficult if she attended his class on reproduction and asked that she please stay away, Elizabeth did not immediately reply.

She wanted to be tactful but at the same time she knew that she must defend her rights. If she were to be a good doctor she must be fully instructed in all phases of her profession.

She spent several hours writing her reply. It was an intelligent, thoughtful letter. She pointed out that she was a registered student, that she wished to learn all she could. Would it make it any easier for him if she took off her bonnet and sat on a back bench?

She ended by saying, "If the male students share your feelings, I will remain away, but I prefer to attend."

When the doctor had read her letter, he stopped her in the hall of the college. He said, "If all my students were actuated by sentiments such as yours, the medical class at Geneva would be a noble one indeed." Would Miss Blackwell wait here in the hall while he put the matter to the students?

She sat in the hall, her hands tightly clasped and cold. She knew that the doctor conducted this particular class with a very broad humor and that the students responded with their own jokes. Maybe this would decide them against her.

The silence inside the classroom deepened Elizabeth's anxiety. Suddenly there was a burst of applause and the door was flung open by the professor. "Come in, come in!" he said heartily. "You stood on your rights and you're entitled to your full tuition."

When she entered, shy and smiling, the young men stood up and gave her a cheer.

Poor patients were often used by the doctors for purposes of demonstration. In her diary Elizabeth wrote, "Dr. Webster sent for me to examine a poor woman in his room. It was a horrible exposure; indecent for any poor woman to be subjected to such torture. She seemed to feel it, poor and ignorant as she was. I felt more than ever the necessity of my mission. But I felt alone. I must work by myself all my life long."

When the summer vacation came she returned to Philadelphia to earn money giving music lessons. She also applied for the post of junior resident at the Almshouse.

The director was incredulous. A woman! He had two thousand inmates—criminals, tramps, orphans, foundlings, prostitutes. No respectable people ever came near the place, even in the name of charity! The stench was appalling, the building itself was falling to pieces.

Elizabeth explained patiently that, as a doctor, she needed experience. She explained it over and over. Stench, poverty, sin—they were all the same in her desire to alleviate suffering. At last the director agreed, shaking his head.

But Elizabeth's few patients did not welcome her. None of them had sunk so low as to accept a woman doctor! Treatments were crude. When a patient had a high fever, a bucket of cold water was doused over him

and his filthy bed. The other junior resident doctors re-
sented her. Patients' charts were hidden so she was obliged
to diagnose what was needed.

Elizabeth's only friend was the chief resident physician, Dr. Benedict. He was a man of compassion who
struggled against the indescribable conditions and did all
he could to get decent food for the inmates. Tea, dark
bread, and a quarter of a pound of bad meat a day was
considered sufficient for paupers and orphans. It was not
surprising that epidemics swept through the buildings.

During a typhus epidemic that summer the staff
worked day and night, and Elizabeth's stamina and de-
votion swept away her last enemy. When the summer was
over she knew all there was to know about typhus—and
that was little enough! She wrote a thesis on it for Dr.
Benedict and took the occasion to urge that intelligent,
compassionate women become nurses—the same cry that
Florence Nightingale was raising in England.

When she returned to Geneva in the fall she found
that she had many friends. The men treated her like
one of themselves. It made her work so much easier that
she felt as though a great load had been lifted from her.
She was not prepared for an enormous hurdle that was
suddenly thrust in her way.

Examinations were to take place in January. As the time
drew nearer and nearer, the trustees were shaken by aw-
ful qualms. It was all very well for a woman to be admitted
to the classes, but how could they dare give her a
diploma?

Once more her friend, Dr. Webster, came to her aid.

"This lady has paid her tuition. She has passed every
course with honors. Let me tell you, gentlemen, if you
hold back, I'll take up a campaign in every medical
journal."

With many misgivings they yielded. Elizabeth's brother Henry promised to come and escort her to the church where the graduation service would be.

Dr. Webster asked her to walk in the commencement procession with her fellow students through the town, but she said, No. She knew that the town, although more friendly, was still watching for unladylike behavior on her part. However she would sit in a pew reserved for the students.

When her name was called to receive her diploma, the president of the college took off his mortarboard to a lady. Elizabeth, smaller and shyer than ever, received the treasured diploma with a little curtsey. Then, impulsively, she turned back to him and said, "I thank you, sir. By the help of the Most High, it shall be the effort of my life to shed honor upon your diploma."

It might seem that the worst was over. Dr. Elizabeth Blackwell was now free to practice medicine. But Elizabeth's hardest days lay before her.

She realized that she must have *more* training than a man. A woman doctor had to be better than the best male physician in the world. Paris was the world center of medical fame in those days. Somehow she had to receive further training in Paris before she would have the least chance in her own country.

In May of that year, 1849, Elizabeth arrived in Paris. She had a letter of introduction to Dr. P. J. Roux.

Dr. Roux was courteous but cautious. He said she could attend his lectures and go with him on his rounds of the hospital wards. But the director-general soon put a stop to that. Two other doctors refused to allow her into their classrooms, although one did offer to look the other way if she put on men's clothes.

Her diploma counted for nothing.

A woman simply could not be accepted as a graduate physician no matter what a diploma said. She discovered the only place that would admit her was the Maternity Hospital. And she could go there only as an apprentice midwife. She agreed.

The other students were young peasant girls, rowdy and good-natured, perfectly content with their limited instruction. Elizabeth, who was already a fully qualified midwife, now made beds and dusted and stood at attention when the doctors made their rounds. She could ask no questions but she watched every move with a practiced eye and made copious notes in the book she always carried.

With the patients she talked tactfully but endlessly, asking them questions with such obvious skill that soon the rollicking young apprentices realized she knew as much as their instructors.

Presently they were asking her for instruction.

Her tact was rewarded. As more and more of the staff became aware that the young American was no novice, they offered her greater facilities. The senior assistant, Dr. Blot, lent her medical books. She taught him English.

When she delivered her first baby, the chief doctor commented dryly that she had the capacity to become the best obstetrician in America. "Study with me for a year." This same man, a few months before, had refused her admittance to the Paris School of Medicine.

But surgery was what she wanted to do. Surgery fascinated her.

She was permitted to watch an hour-long operation. The patience and manual dexterity and anatomical knowledge of the surgeon convinced her that it was the branch of medicine which interested her the most. She would concentrate all her attention on her surgical skill.

Then a dreadful accident happened. While syringing the eyes of a baby suffering from an infection, some of the liquid flew into her own eyes. She paid no attention and went on with her work. The next day she could hardly see.

The whole hospital rallied to her. Dr. Blot asked to be relieved of all duties so that he might care for her alone. When he knew that the sight had been lost in one of her eyes, he did not have the courage to tell her. But Elizabeth found out for herself.

For two days she yielded to unspeakable grief. Surgery would now be out of the question. Dr. Blot told her that if one eye were removed, he thought he could save the other. He performed the delicate operation and she, badly shaken, faced life again.

By now she had many friends and admirers in the medical fraternity. She was offered the chance of graduate study at St. Bartholomew's Hospital in London, one of the oldest hospitals in the world.

Before her arrival, the dean gave the students a very moving account of her fight for a medical education and the accident which had affected her sight. When she came into the amphitheater for her first lecture, the young Englishmen rose—as had her American colleagues at Geneva—and gave her a cheer.

Her accident made her search more deeply for the source of her confidence. She had been steadfast, unselfish, profoundly motivated. She was also a good doctor. As she followed the senior doctors from ward to ward she was fully competent to criticize—silently—some of their methods and was also well aware how much guesswork was involved in the "science" she had adopted.

Her months in England were happy ones. She grew to know many of the vivid men and women who were changing history. Florence Nightingale and she became friends and admirers. She met Lady Byron and the great actress and abolitionist Fanny Kemble. She even dallied with the notion of staying in England. After all, it was her birthplace. But when she discovered that her own fight for a medical education had already made things easier for women in the United States, she decided that her practice must begin at home.

She was thirty years old when she returned to New York: Dr. Elizabeth Blackwell.

"Doctor" Elizabeth—it was almost like a curse. No landlady wanted her. Real estate agents would not sell or rent to her if a brass plate on her door with "Dr. Blackwell" was her goal.

She went from hospital to hospital presenting her glowing letters from European doctors. Everywhere she was treated with contempt.

She wrote to her sister: "A blank wall of social and professional antagonism faces a woman physician—a situation of singular and painful loneliness, leaving her without support, respect or professional counsel."

She knew desperately that she must find a place where she could begin a professional life. Perhaps if she paid more . . . She had little money and no prospects, but when she was shown a floor at 44 University Place in New York City she took it. The rent was far beyond her means. She was not allowed to put out a sign. Her landlady refused to take messages, but from this step must come her future.

She could not go out into the highways and byways calling for patients. After a few weeks she invested some of her meager funds in an advertisement in the New York *Tribune*. The editor of the *Tribune* was Horace Greeley, an antislavery man and a firm believer in woman's rights. In her advertisement she gave her credentials and her desire "to practice in every department of her profession."

No patients came.

She tried a different tack. Knowing the appalling biologic ignorance of girls about themselves, she announced a series of lectures designed to cut through this darkness. She called it, "The Laws of Life with Special Reference to the Physical Education of Girls."

This was in some ways more challenging than a doctor's nameplate. It took very broad-minded people to feel that any information about their own bodies or about childbearing should be given to unmarried girls.

A handful of women attended the first lecture. Most of them were Quakers. Elizabeth pleaded for enlightenment and healthy activity for girls, an end to the prudishness and false information.

One of the women was the wife of a printer. This remarkable man invited Elizabeth to become his family physician. Slowly, inch by inch, she began to gain a foothold.

Most of her patients were Quakers—those wonderful people who believed in the equality of all before God—and several of them came to her support. Horace Greeley used every occasion to point to her as an example women should follow.

However, hostility and abuse continued to be more familiar than praise. Every step was a fight. She could not afford to relax for a moment. Her family were, of course, behind her in every possible way, but they lived in Ohio. When her sister Emily arrived in New York it was like an answer to prayer.

Emily, red-haired, attractive, also wanted to be a doctor. Elizabeth's heart lightened.

She encouraged Emily in every way, knowing that Emily would find out the discouraging things by herself. To the astonishment of both sisters, Bellevue, the largest hospital in New York, agreed to give Emily training. Elizabeth had made this possible by her own courageous fight.

In order to have the use of hospital facilities, Elizabeth had applied repeatedly to the New York Dispensary for a staff position, only to be refused "because a lady would not promote the harmonious working of the institution." Disappointed but undefeated, she resolved to establish her own dispensary.

One of the poorest, most brutal and squalid neighborhoods in New York was around Tompkins Square. There Elizabeth found a reeking, filthy room. She herself threw out the worst rubbish in the room, scrubbed the floors, whitewashed the walls. Her Quaker friends sprang to her assistance. They contributed curtains and furnishings, medicine and drugs. In March, 1853, the New York Dispensary for Indigent Women and Children opened its doors in a section of the city where no male doctor wished to venture.

From the squalid shadows, from the desperate hovels, women and children watched Elizabeth, small, neat and smiling. But none came as her patients. She soon realized that she must become familiar to them before they would trust her.

One day a mother brought her child. Elizabeth diagnosed its illness correctly and made the child well. Another mother came with *her* child. The woman had come more out of desperation than hope, and went away with Elizabeth's compassionate remedies.

Elizabeth was drawn deeper and deeper into the desperate, brutalized life of the neighborhood. She became convinced that cleanliness was the first law of medicine. In this neighborhood of poverty and violence, babies were born and children played among indescribable filth. She knew the situation in all its details, for she went boldly into the hovels when a patient was too sick or drunk to come to her.

Drunkenness was even more prevalent than sickness. Women in childbirth were drunk, men were drunk day and night, even children were drunk. Alcohol seemed the only way to blot out the terrible misery of their lives. Yet Elizabeth was not afraid. Emergency calls came in the middle of the night. With one thought—"God is with me!"—she took her small satchel of medicine and plunged into the black alleys where no policemen or male doctors dared to go.

From these patients Elizabeth could expect no money, and as yet her well-to-do patients could be counted on her fingers. Abusive anonymous letters, coming as regularly as the dawn, were her chief contact with the rest of the world. She threw the letters away, but they emphasized her loneliness.

Emily, who had gone to Rush College in Chicago for her final training and diploma, promised to come to her help as soon as she graduated. Elizabeth counted the days. Emily had. been as fine and quick a student as she herself. On the eve of Emily's graduation she was told that she would not be given her diploma. The Illinois

Society of Medicine had just passed a resolution condemning Rush College for teaching her.

Emily wasted no time in recrimination. She sent pressing letters to other colleges, asking them to honor her credits. It was a nerve-racking time. At last Western Reserve University in Cleveland agreed to admit her at once, and she graduated with high honors.

But still Elizabeth had to wait. Both sisters knew that Emily's value would be increased if she had special training in gynecology. With her diploma still clutched in her hand, the younger sister sailed for England and joined the staff of Sir James Young Simpson in Edinburgh.

Elizabeth's own professional needs had become acute, and in her personal life she badly needed love and companionship. Marriage seemed out of the question at the moment. Yet the terrible loneliness she had foreseen as a student enveloped her day and night.

That autumn she decided to adopt a child. She selected a delicate, forlorn little Irish orphan named Katherine. Her love for the child, and the child's love for her, restored her spirit.

Elizabeth and Emily planned to establish a hospital for women, staffed by women, and with its own medical school.

The hospital was not such a wild dream as it might have seemed a few years before. A school for women medical students had been opened in Philadelphia, another one in Boston. Neither gave complete training, but they broke an impasse. New York Hospital had admitted eight women students.

Before the year was out a young Polish woman, Marie Zackrzewska, appealed to Elizabeth as Elizabeth had appealed to others: Take me—give me training!

Marie had come to America to study medicine: all she had been allowed to do was embroider hats for less than one dollar a day. She was sharp, keen, intelligent, and had had training as a midwife.

Elizabeth gave her affection and encouraged her to go to Western Reserve for her training, then return and join forces.

Emily was on her way back to New York, having refused Florence Nightingale's invitation to work with her in the Crimea; and Elizabeth, Emily, and soon Marie would be a formidable trio.

In order to lose no time, Elizabeth applied to New York State for a charter for her hospital. To her surprise and joy it was granted. To her even greater surprise and joy, several prominent men in New York offered to act as trustees, and a number of surgeons and physicians agreed to serve as consultants. Elizabeth Blackwell, the first American woman to receive a medical diploma, had moved history forward a second inch!

She was under no illusions that women doctors would have an easy time, but certainly they would never have quite so *hard* a time again.

Elizabeth needed $5,000 to start her hospital. Goodwill proved easier to raise than money.

The whole country was in the throes of a depression. Talk of Civil War was in the air, though it was only 1854. Yet Elizabeth knew that her idea could not be stopped.

Her Quaker friends organized bazaars and sewing circles in the interest of the hospital. Marie, graduating from Western Reserve rushed up to Boston to get the support of the famous abolitionists who were masters of the art of wringing money from stones. William Lloyd Garrison and Ralph Waldo Emerson promised to do what they could. The sum of $650 was raised at an Antislavery Fair.

In New York another six hundred dollars came from a second Antislavery Fair. Friends in England sent money.

Soon after New Year's Day, 1855, Elizabeth paid two years' rent for a building on Bleecker Street—a building owned by a Dutch family named Roosevelt.

Emily, home at last, was a little alarmed by the speed and scope of Elizabeth's undertakings. But Elizabeth showed her how carefully the plans had been thought out.

The front and back drawing rooms were turned into six-bed wards. On the second floor additional beds were placed, and the master bedroom became the operating theater. On the third floor and attic were bedrooms for students and nurses.

Elizabeth hated the cold air of institutions, so she made the atmosphere as homelike as possible. Flowers, attractive colors, comfortable furniture, were everywhere. Her brothers, Henry and Samuel, arrived in New York at this time to give what help they could.

Henry was about to marry Lucy Stone. Their courtship had been a rather unusual one, for Lucy was indeed an unusual woman. Henry had heard her lecture on women's rights and had been so impressed that he immediately asked permission to call on her. He was chagrined by her refusal but persisted in his efforts to meet her. It was not until their mutual friend, William Lloyd Garrison, intervened, however, that she agreed to see him. Despite Garrison's high recommendations Lucy remained aloof until Henry's hazardous involvement in the rescue of a fugitive slave convinced her of the sincerity of his ideals.

Samuel was already married. His wife was Antoinette Brown, the first woman ordained as a minister. She, too, was a unique woman, as much interested in prison reform as in women's rights and the abolition of slavery.

Elizabeth planned to open the hospital on May 12, 1857, the birthday of Florence Nightingale. It was a festive day. The Virginia Reel was danced by all her famous guests, young and old, and then the hospital was inspected from attic to basement.

Not only was it well equipped but it guaranteed a training that women students could get no other place in the world. Elizabeth was director; Emily was surgeon; Marie was resident physician.

These were grand titles, but they could not conceal the fact that Elizabeth, Emily, and Marie were also nurses, bookkeepers, and cleaning women.

Patients began to arrive almost as soon as the hospital opened. They were asked to pay four dollars a week if they could afford it, but many were admitted free.

In seven months the three women treated over nine hundred cases.

They had to learn to communicate with Italians, Poles, Ukrainians, Gaelic-speaking Irish. They had to learn to fight their enemies by conciliating them.

When one patient died, a mob gathered, crying, "You killed her!" The situation was desperate, but an Irish laborer whose wife had been treated by Elizabeth managed to roar above the noise that patients died in men's hospitals also.

When a second patient died—a patient who had been admitted after all hope had gone—Elizabeth succeeded in getting word to a doctor at Bellevue before the mob arrived. He came and shouted to the crowd that he would order an autopsy and twelve of them might be present to see that no negligence had been involved.

Elizabeth knew better than anyone else how closely and coldly the work of the hospital was being scrutinized. She knew that the hospital and staff still had more enemies than friends. Emily, about to perform an operation, had to wait for an hour while the male surgeon who was to act as consultant argued with a colleague the propriety of assisting a woman doctor.

But the compensations were many. During the first year four women medical students came to the hospital for the practical experience they could gain nowhere else. In the following year over three thousand patients were treated, and Elizabeth established an out-patient department that was far in advance of its time.

No one knew better than she the desperate home conditions to which her patients returned. She tried to give them a continuing care. When protests were made that she was going faster than public opinion, she answered, "Public opinion should be made, not followed."

When the Civil War broke out, Elizabeth's first thought paralleled that of Dorothea Dix: women nurses. She called a meeting of her directors, but the directors were not the only people who attended—uninvited women swarmed in.

The meeting ended with resolutions which attempted to coordinate all volunteer nursing efforts and at the same time establish high standards of qualification. Elizabeth, always quiet and reserved, knew that she and a handful of women like her were the custodians of women's professional standing.

She had a real genius for organizing, and she would probably have done a better job than Dorothea Dix to whom the assignment was given. But the two women worked closely together bearing the brunt of Army Medical Corps disapproval. Those nursing candidates selected by Elizabeth were trained briefly at the Infirmary or at

Bellevue and then were sent on to Dorothea Dix in Washington.

As a result of her activities during the war Elizabeth was given a charter for her medical college. Now the problem had a new twist. Women's interest was growing by leaps and bounds, but increased interest and opportunity had not resulted in more adequate preparation. In many medical colleges a prospective doctor, male as well as female, received less than a year's training.

Elizabeth dreaded half knowledge more than anything. She required entrance examinations for her college and a full three-year training course with plenty of practical experience.

One of the most remarkable things about Elizabeth Blackwell was that she never lost her profound insights. To her the work was a vital mission to mankind. It was an expression of love shown in practical ways. Her experience confirmed her belief that an entire community's health of mind and body was indispensable to an individual's well-being.

She became interested in Christian Socialism because she felt that the complexities of social life required care and planning in order that everyone could lead a decent life. Children became one of her primary concerns.

When a French admirer gave her nine thousand dollars to be used as she saw fit—to build a convalescent home for women and children or to build open-air playgrounds or to develop techniques of instruction in home and child care for desperately poor mothers—Elizabeth seized on the chance to work right in the homes.

She wanted every child to have the best chance in the world.

She understood herself very well. She was not the

born doctor that Emily was, or Marie. "I work chiefly in principles," Elizabeth said to a friend. The moral ends concerned her. She loved freedom. She acted upon it. She required it for others.

She lived to be a very old woman, nearly ninety. Through all those years she taught, wrote, agitated for a healthier and more generous attitude toward the poor, the weak, the sick. All her life she remained a visionary, convinced that a material explanation of things was not the whole story.

What the whole story was she did not know, but she acted to the limits of her faith—and then beyond.

FIVE

Harriet Tubman

BROWN BROTHERS

THESE women who fought for freedom from big-
otry were spared the worst indignity of all—enslavement because of having a dark skin.

A century ago a man or woman or child whose skin
was not white could be bought and sold like a plow or a
loaf of bread. He had no rights of any kind. He could be
used in business transactions like a horse or a cow. He
could be mortgaged like a house or furntiure. He could
not marry legally. His children did not belong to him but
to the master who could sell them at will.

He was not allowed to read or write. He had no protection whatever against brutality except his monetary
value, and even that value was badly affected if he was not
docile. He could be beaten to death or killed in any way,
with only the most perfunctory protest from law offi-
cers who were usually slavemasters themselves.

To talk to a slave woman of women's right to vote or
to become a doctor was laughable. *She* was not even
allowed the right to herself!

As the economy of the South became increasingly dependent on cotton, sugar, rice, and tobacco, slavery became
more and more inhuman. Most plantation owners were
convinced that slave labor was essential to the economic
survival of the agricultural South.

While many Southeners deplored these conditions—for
only a fraction were slaveowners—not only the economy
of the South but its politics and whole social structure

depended on slavery, and therefore slave laws determined almost every aspect of life.

It was an extraordinary situation, and it is not surprising that only the violence of a civil war could break the vicious circle.

Harriet Tubman was a Negro child, a slave, born to slave parents and owned by a Maryland master. She was born in 1821, the year of the great slave uprising in South Carolina led by a black man, Denmark Vesey. All through that year, and for many years to come, Vesey's name rang through the slave cabins. His exploit frightened some slaves because masters became harsher, but it excited others to hope. As a very small child, Harriet was taught to sing a song that Vesey had made popular:

> Go down, Moses,
> Way down to Egypt land!
> And tell old Pharaoh
> To let my people go!

It was a dangerous song to sing. It had to be sung under the breath even when no white man was around. But in the years to come, it became Harriet's song.

Harriet was a scrawny, bright little girl. At the age of six she was hired out to a woman who beat her, fed her scraps, and did not let her sleep enough. When the woman finally brought her back to the master as "not worth anything," Harriet's back was a mass of scars from her beatings.

The second time she was hired she was a little older and wiser. She worked in the fields, which she liked. Her father was hired out to the same person, and he taught her strange things—how to move silently through the woods so that no one could hear her, how to recognize edible berries and roots. It was as though he expected her to escape sometime, and he wanted her to be prepared. Those run-aways who did not succeed were punished terribly.

In the whisperings of the cabin Harriet had also learned that a mysterious system of help for those same runaways was called the Underground Railroad. It was really a long line of friends, white and Negro, stretching into the South, who passed fugitives from one hiding place to the next until they reached the North. It was very dangerous for both the fugitive and his friends if they were caught.

When Harriet was eleven, she put on a bandanna as a sign that she was grown up. A Negro girl of eleven was sup-posed to do a woman's work, although childhood was a luxury most had never known. Harriet began to think about the future in vague terms, mostly in terms of escape and freedom for her whole family. Some of her sisters had already been sold. Harriet had watched them, fastened together with chains, stumble down the road toward the Deep South. Her mother had not dared to weep, al-though she knew she would never see them again.

That year Virginia, a state practically next door to Maryland, shook to the sounds of another slave uprising led by Nat Turner. All over the South controls tightened. Slaves, lying awake in their cabins, could hear the pound-ing of horses' hoofs night after night. "The patrol," they would whisper to each other, "out looking for runaway slaves."

One day when Harriet was working the field of her master she realized that one of the slave men was edging closer and closer to the woods. Presently she knew that he was trying to make a break for freedom. The overseer realized it at the same time. Harriet moved quickly and succeeded in blocking the overseer for the moment it took the slave to get out of sight. In a rage, the overseer flung a metal weight after the man and struck Harriet in the forehead.

For hours she lay unconscious. The news that she had helped a slave escape spread through the plantation. Slaves crept in the dark to see her lying on a pallet tended by her fearful mother. A slave who had helped another escape had lost all value to his master. He was a liability who must be gotten rid of as quickly as possible, before he infected the other slaves.

While Harriet was still unconscious her master tried to sell her. Buyers came to look at her, but when they saw the injured girl they laughed. Buy *her*? No man was such a fool.

For many months Harriet lay in a stupor. When she recovered and was able to work again, unconsciousness would come on her without warning. In the middle of a sentence, or as she was walking or working, her head would jerk forward and she would lose consciousness. When she opened her eyes she would finish her sentence or continue her action, but in the interval she was completely helpless.

Suddenly her master died. The heir was a child, and by the master's will the estate was to be held together until the child came of age.

Harriet was hired out because she was as strong as a man. One day as she was working in the field near the road, a white woman driving a wagon stopped. She watched Harriet for a few moments before she spoke to her. She seemed to understand the meaning of that terrible scar on Harriet's forehead. She said softly, "If you ever want any help, let me know."

That was all she said, and Harriet asked no questions.

Within the year the heir to the plantation died. Immediately the rumors spread that all the slaves would be sold.
Panic followed. When Harriet saw the white woman again,
she mentioned her fear. The woman nodded and softly
repeated what she had already said.

Two more of Harriet's sisters were sold, and Harriet
knew that she could wait no longer. Escape—with this
hole in her forehead and the constant danger of unconsciousness? She knew she would need help. One day as
the waterboy gave her a dip of water in the field, he
whispered that she had just been sold to a slavetrader.

She had to move without delay. The trader would
collect her the next morning as his gang moved from one
plantation to another. She whispered, "Lord, I've got to
hold steady on to You, and You've got to see me through."

That night she wrapped a little food in a handkerchief
and started for the house where the white woman lived.
It might be a trap, but she had to take the risk. Years later
she wrote, "I had reasoned this out in my mind; there
was one of two things I had the *right* to: liberty or death.
If I could not have one I would have the other, for no
man should take me alive. I should fight for my liberty
as long as my strength lasted."

When she finally knocked on the door, the woman welcomed her without surprise. She wasted no words. She was
a "conductor" on the Underground Railroad. She told Harriet exactly how to find the next "station," where friends
would feed her and guide her on the next lap of the
way North.

In the black of the night Harriet set out. She knew she
had to reach that first station by morning, for the patrol
would be looking for her the moment the alarm was raised.
The scar on her forehead would be her worst enemy.

By dawn she had reached the first stop. Everything happened as the woman had said. Another white woman fed her, then gave her a broom and told her to work in the yard. This was as good a disguise as any, for a working Negro would not cause any suspicion.

That night her new friend's husband hid her in a wagon and started off down the road. Harriet always marveled at her trust. He might be delivering her back to her master for all she knew, but somehow she felt these people were doing God's work and would not betray her.

Before dawn the man stopped his wagon. He told her to hurry along by the river until she reached the next station, which he described to her carefully. He warned her against all roads by daylight.

It took her nearly two weeks to travel the ninety miles into the free state of Pennsylvania. She had been hidden in a haystack, rowed up a river, hidden by free Negroes in a potato hole, concealed in an attic, and at last delivered into freedom.

"I looked at my hands to see if I was the same person. There was such a glory over everything . . . that I felt like I was in heaven."

These were not grandiose words. Harriet, like many other great people, had a deep and simple faith that a spiritual power was controlling her movements.

She reached Philadelphia, which was a nerve center of the Underground Railroad. The "terminus" was found in a room in the Lebanon Seminary. William Still, a Negro, was in charge, aided and supported by several other Negroes and Quakers of the city. They did business twenty-four hours a day.

Harriet had caught a vivid glimpse of the careful, accurate, almost infallible work of rescuing fugitives. She told herself that if the slaves in the South knew that running away need not be a hit-or-miss business, they would leave by the hundreds. Everyone had to be free! The imagination, the courage, the faith, that made freedom a living experience filled her heart with joy.

She found a job in a hotel and saved every penny she could. She was determined to return to Maryland and bring out her parents. But one day, when she was in the "terminus" office with William Still, she learned that a message had come from the "conductor" in Cambridge, Maryland. He needed a foolproof means of transporting "two large bales of wool and two small." He was especially worried about the last stage of the journey from Baltimore to Philadelphia because of the "two little bales."

Harriet understood that "bales of wool" referred to adults and children, but to her absolute astonishment she heard the name Bowley mentioned.

"That's my brother-in-law's name!" she cried, and her eager questions brought out the fact that "the bales of wool" were indeed her own family: one of her sisters, her sister's two children and her husband, a free Negro.

"I'll go!" Harriet said promptly. Mr. Still replied with an emphatic "No." Placards describing Harriet and offering rewards were still being circulated.

"The conductor who meets the family in Baltimore will have to lead them openly through the streets of the city."

But Harriet persisted. "I'm the one who's going to Baltimore," she said stubbornly. Mr. Still yielded. He gave her instructions and a disguise.

The Bowleys, exhausted and trembling, were brought into a warm, sweet-smelling kitchen in Baltimore. A Negro man got up from a chair and said, "Mary!"

Mary Bowley did not recognize this "man" as her sister

Harriet until she took off her battered man's hat. Then there were tears and embraces.

The Bowleys and Harriet remained hidden in the house for a week till the hue and cry died down. There were endless talks about the inalienable rights of freedom and how to make certain an escape did not fail. The Bowleys' escape had been extremely dramatic.

Mary and the two children had actually been in the possession of the slave auctioneer, locked in the slave pen, before John Bowley had discovered their danger.

John went in desperation to a Quaker friend and they formed a daring plot.

John arrived at the office of the slave market with a large official envelope. He handed it to the guard. The guard read, "Send the women and children to the inn. I have a buyer." It was signed with the auctioneer's name.

The auctioneer was a stranger to the guard, so he accepted Bowley's word that he was the auctioneer's servant and shoved out Mary and the two children.

John Bowley gave no sign of knowing his wife. He wanted to run with them, hide, but instead he led them at a careful walking pace. He was terrified that the auctioneer might appear at any moment.

His wife was in tears, believing that in some way John was betraying them. After a long agonizing walk during which he could give her no comfort, they came to a quiet street. He looked around carefully, opened a gate, and said, "Quick now! Run!" A side door of the house opened, and the four vanished from sight.

They remained hidden in their Quaker host's attic till dark. Late that night they were concealed in a wagon and driven to a river. John, who knew how to sail a boat, was given instructions. When he drew near Baltimore he was to watch for two lights, one blue, one yellow. At dawn he saw the lights faintly gleaming. A white woman was waiting for them. He gave the password, "A friend with friends." She hid them in her wagon and drove them to the other side of town. All day they stayed out of sight in a stable, and with night they darted through the shadows into the kitchen and to reunion with Harriet.

At the end of the week Harriet brought them safely through Baltimore and up the secret road to Philadelphia. She was exhilarated. Freedom was such a living fact that she would never let it go. The road from Baltimore to Philadelphia was less than a hundred miles, and in the months that followed she became as familiar with it as with the streets of those cities.

But her exhilaration was cut short. The year was 1850 and the Fugitive Slave Law was passed by Congress. This law altered the entire picture. Everyone on the Underground Railroad, every abolitionist, was studying the law as though his life depended on it; and, in fact, this was the case.

It was a monstrous law, a concession made to the slaveowners by Northern politicians who hoped in this way to bridge the widening gulf between the North and the South. With this law no Negro whether born in the North or a fugitive was really safe.

The identification of a Negro could be made on the affidavit of a slavecatcher without any effort to prove his word. The Negro could offer no defense or testify for himself. The fee of the commissioner who settled the case was ten dollars if he found for the master and only five dollars if he freed the Negro. If a federal agent in any way hampered the seizure of the Negro, he was fined one thousand dollars. If a fugitive escaped, with or without his aid, the federal agent was held responsible for the entire value claimed for the Negro. Bystanders were required to assist in the recapture of a fugitive. Anyone convicted of aiding an escaped slave was liable to a fine of a thousand dollars or imprisonment for six months. The fugitive himself could be shot without question or sent to the Deep South where he would have less chance of another escape.

Even free Negroes, with identity papers, were not really safe. As for fugitives like Harriet and the fifty thousand like her in the North, they could be seized at any moment. There was no true safety south of Canada.

Free Negroes left northern towns by the hundreds, heading for Canada, although Negro leaders urged their people to stay and resist. The Underground Railroad became more active than ever. Passengers arrived day and night, and now the escape routes had to extend straight across the North. More and more people who had hitherto been aloof were lending a hand. The cruelty of the new law was so outrageous that many believed it their duty to disobey it.

Harriet's own danger increased of course—and also her eagerness. Her whole point of view broadened. Originally she had dreamed only of saving her family. Now anyone with a black skin had a claim on her courage.

In the spring of 1851 she went down the long dark road to Maryland and brought out three men. In the fall she collected a small group of slaves from the neighborhood of her old home and led them safely into Philadelphia, where they were turned over to other "conductors" for the journey north.

Both times she talked about freedom to every Negro she met. For those bold enough to strike out for themselves, she explained the route carefully. She had a strong, clear way of talking.

As her returns became more frequent a legend grew up around her. She was called Moses. In the dark of the night the slaves waited to hear her low song, "Go down, Moses, and tell old Pharaoh to let my people go."

Not only had the slaves made her a legend but the white masters as well. Who was this Moses? What man dared to storm the fortress of slavery? Harriet chuckled. Let them think her a man and she would break a few more chains of slavery.

Harriet, like Elizabeth Blackwell, had convictions and insights that ran counter to practical good sense. Both believed God talked to them. Almost all of Harriet's trips were made in response to what Harriet believed was a divine command: "So-and-so is in danger," or "So-and-so needs you." She always found this was true.

She required absolute obedience of those who came away with her—silence, promptness. She had the strength to lift a man in her arms and run with him if he did not move quickly enough when danger loomed. She had the sharp intelligence to meet every emergency, and proof of this lay in the fact that, in nineteen trips into Maryland, she never lost a single slave of the three hundred she led to freedom. She had the iron courage also to carry a pistol wherever she went and threaten to use it if any of her charges showed timidity.

The sound of a horse galloping in the dark meant a quick concealment by the side of the road. The sudden wail of a slave baby meant an extra dose of paragoric so that it lay quietly in its mother's arms. Invariably she had to dominate the fears of her charges and never let them see a moment's hesitation on her part.

Although she was often fearful and more often exhausted, she never let the frightened and weary fugitives see this. She had to be heroic, calm, in complete control, twenty-four hours a day. Mere bodily safety was only one part of her mission. She opened the eyes of the Negroes to many new responsibilities they would face. As they traveled she instructed, comforted, sang, gave them an education in what it meant to be a free people—the hardships, the glories.

She usually chose a Saturday night for the escape because a day then intervened before an advertisement for the runaway could appear. Her routes varied. Sometimes she went west toward the mountains. Other times she went toward Wilmington where her good friend Thomas Garrett (who before he died had passed more than three thousand fugitives over the underground line) was always waiting for her.

She had to be prepared for any danger leaping out of a bush. Remember, this was the woman who, at any moment, at the peak of any crisis, might lose consciousness because of that old injury to her head. But she believed God guided and protected her, and her actions were always shaped by this faith and her lightning-quick wits.

Once, riding north on a train, she heard her name spoken. Frozen with caution, she looked under the edge of her sunbonnet and saw a tall man reading aloud an advertisement to a companion. . . . A runaway slave named Harriet Tubman with a scar on her forehead was worth the incredible reward of five thousand dollars.

Harriet kept her head lowered until she reached the next station. There she took a train going south, knowing that a Negro woman going in that direction as fast as the wheels could turn would not be suspected. She made her way to the town near her old home and did not resume her journey north until the hue and cry had died down.

The reward for her finally reached $40,000.

To be a woman *and* a Negro were twin handicaps in those days, but Harriet's magnificence as a human being overcame obstacles and won her a host of loyal friends.

As the shadows of a civil war deepened, she sometimes found that a station was no longer open. Once she arrived with eleven fugitives at a trusted hiding place. But the "conductor," seeing twelve desperate and weary runaways, slammed the door in their faces. "Too many! Too many! My place was searched last week!"

She stayed with these eleven all the way to Canada. The trip took almost a month. In Canada she remained with them through the winter, helping them find jobs, build houses, meet the terrible onslaughts of a cold they had never known. A small community was established to which she could bring other runaways. In Canada Negroes had legal rights. In Canada black men became county officials and members of school boards. Their children went to school.

For the next six years she went into Maryland every fall and spring and brought out bondmen. Each trip was in obedience to what she termed that "inner voice." At one point her dreams directed her to three of her brothers: Ben, John and William Henry. She knew how difficult it would be to reach them, as they belonged to different masters. So she wrote the following letter to a free Negro friend in Maryland named Jacob Jackson:

> Read my letter to the old folks and give my love to them, and tell my brothers to be always watching unto prayer, and when the good old ship of Zion comes along to be ready to step on board.
>   WILLIAM HENRY JACKSON.

Jacob Jackson had an adopted son, William Henry, who had moved legally to the North. But William Henry Jackson had neither brothers nor old folk, so Jacob Jackson had to read the letter for another meaning. He knew "Moses," he knew her brothers, he knew "the good ship Zion" meant escape. He interpreted the letter correctly, *"Warn my brothers to be ready to leave."*

However Jacob Jackson was not able to read this letter in leisurely privacy. He had to read it swiftly under the eyes of a white postmaster who, as a matter of course, opened any letters addressed to free Negroes. The postmaster also knew that William Henry Jackson had no kin except the free Negro, Jacob.

Jacob pretended great stupidity. "It can't be meant for me nohow!" Then he hurried as fast as he could to get word to Harriet's three brothers. All of them wondered how she knew of their danger: the three brothers had been sold to a trader who was to pick them up the day after Christmas.

Harriet came for them on December 23. On the 29th, William Still wrote in his record book, "Moses arrived with six passengers." She had brought not only her three brothers but a girl whom her brother William wished to marry and two other slave men.

Harriet's train was never derailed. She never lost a passenger. Many of her friends in the North tried to explain the reason for this—her courage, her resourcefulness, her experience. They seemed reluctant to give it the mysterious quality of faith which Harriet gave it. She believed that God was directing her and no one could make her believe differently. She believed that her instructions came in her vivid dreams. In June, 1857, her nights were filled with dreams of her parents, Rit and Ben. All day she lived with the picture she had seen in her dreams—her parents in danger, about to be sold.

For years she had wanted to bring Rit and Ben into

freedom. But she had hesitated, for they were old and the kind of travel she required—forced marches through the woods, chin-high wading through rivers—demanded youth and agility. How could she get them off safely? How?

But because she had faith she started South. She had no idea what she would do. She made her way at night to her parents' cabin. She had not seen them for five years.

Her mother welcomed her with tears and said that Ben was being questioned day and night about the escape of a slave. The white men did not let him alone. They threatened to get rid of him, for any slave suspected of aiding a fugitive was a danger to the whole plantation.

When her father returned to the cabin, Harriet took him aside. "Where can I find a horse?" she asked.

He pursed his lips. So many slaves had been escaping that horses were no longer being left in pastures at night. But he remembered Dollie Mae, an old "critter" a mile down the road at the next plantation.

"I'll get her," Harriet whispered. "You get together food and be ready."

In the starlit night she found the old horse lying down asleep. She roused her, got her to her feet, talked sweetly to her, wondering whether the old horse would have the strength to carry the old people to safety.

She still needed a wagon and some sort of harness. She tied the horse in the woods and slipped quietly into the yard back of the old master's barn. Sure enough, there was the wagon she remembered—hardly ever used because it was too small and rickety. Still moving like a ghost in the dark of the stable, she found a harness. Just as she was leaving she had a terrible fright. A slave she had never seen before suddenly appeared in the doorway. He stared at her without a word. Harriet put her finger to her lips, slipped past him and melted into the night.

She still had to bring the horse to the wagon, harness them together. Would the unknown slave give an alarm? She had to trust. Perhaps he was watching from the dark. She did not know. She managed to get the horses harnessed and hitched, and no alarm was raised. Quietly, quietly, she drove to the woods again and went back on foot for her parents.

Her father would not be separated from his old broadax. Her mother would not leave without her feather tick. Rit, weeping with nerves, was hoisted into the wagon and made comfortable on the feather tick. Ben climbed up beside Harriet. With scarcely a sound they moved down the road, the slow old horse doing her best.

When day came, they slept, hidden in a deep woods. Three nights later Harriet had gotten them miraculously to Thomas Garrett's in Wilmington.

From Wilmington the journey was safer and easier, for friends took charge. All the way to Canada loving hands passed them on.

When they reached Canada, Harriet knew that her own way of life would have to change. She was now responsible for these old people of hers. They would be helpless, alone, in the cold of Canada. Although the United States was filled with danger for young Negroes, she believed that some town in upper New York State, settled and civilized but close to the border, would be safe for such old ones. She thought back over the stops on the underground line The little town of Auburn came to mind again and again.

She borrowed money and bought a small house in Auburn and settled her parents in comfort and safety.

That same year she met John Brown. He told her of his

intention to free as many slaves as he could reach. He called her "General Tubman," for he considered her one of the greatest warriors in the antislavery ranks. He wanted all all the advice and help she could give. She instantly loved and admired a man with such a dream of freedom, but she was afraid for him. His plans were impractical in too many details. Yet she helped.

John Brown had made a great effort to talk to her because her fame had reached far and wide. The *National Antislavery Standard,* a well-read newspaper, commented at this time on a convention of slave masters being held near Harriet's old home in Maryland.

> The operations of the Underground Railroad on the Maryland border within the last few years have been so extensive that in some neighborhoods the whole slave population have made their escape, and the convention is the result of the general panic on the part of the owners.

Harriet's name was not mentioned, but every reader, white or Negro, mentally supplied it.

All over the North antislavery meetings were attracting vast crowds. Harriet was a coveted speaker.

She did not like this public speaking but she saw it as part of her job. She needed money for her work. She knew that freedom had to be stirred in the hearts of people. Often she shared the platform with famous men, white and colored. Harriet, short, muscular, black as night, dressed in a gray gown with lace at her throat and jet buttons down the bodice, was frequently the only woman. She told of her escapes, told them simply, undramatically, but her vivid language and her deep, beautiful voice made the dangerous journeys as real to these people as their own safe journeys home.

To Harriet the greatest miracle of all were the free men and women who endangered their lives and properties for the sake of the slaves. She told of being trapped once in a swamp by a posse of white men. She and her passengers did not know which way to turn. She said, "Lord, I'm going to hold steady on to You."

As dusk came and the patrol was still shouting in the distance, closing in on the swamp, she saw a man walking up and down the edge of the swamp. He was a stranger. He wore the broad-brimmed hat of the Quaker, but slave agents sometimes disguised themselves as Quakers. Harriet crept as close as she could. She saw his lips moving, though he never turned in the direction of the swamp. She strained to hear. He was saying, "My wagon stands in the barnyard right across the way. The horse is in the stable. The harness hangs on a nail."

He repeated the words several times. Then he turned abruptly and disappeared. How had he known where to walk? How did he know she had heard?

After dark, Harriet crept out of the swamp and slithered her way to the yard. There was the wagon. She made sure no spy was concealed in it, for the traps devised by slave masters were very ingenious. She found the horse, harness, and a bundle of food. She got her passengers safely through the cordon of the patrol.

That same year, 1859, John Brown led the insurrection at Harper's Ferry, failed, and was hanged. Harriet wept. Although she felt he had not used his means well, she marveled at his courage and his love of humanity. His death made her feel that she was not doing enough. It was all very well to lead runaways through the blackness of a southern night, but the North needed rousing as well.

She stopped one night in Troy, New York, on her way to Boston. A large crowd around the courthouse caught her attention. What was happening? A fugitive Negro had been seized, was being taken before the commissioner, and would be returned automatically to slavery.

Harriet did not pause for a moment. She saw the struggling young Negro in the grip of half a dozen police. She forced her way through the crowd until she stood beside him. Then she caught hold of a small boy and whispered urgently, "Go out in the street and holler 'Fire!' as loud as you can."

The child nodded and slipped away. She heard his voice, she heard other voices, she heard the firebells begin to ring. The police were still holding on to their prisoner, waiting for the commissioner, when the new excitement made them loosen their grip. Harriet seized the young man's hand and with her muscular arm delivered a blow at the nearest policeman, knocking him down by this surprise attack. She and the young Negro fled down the steps, stumbled, fell.

In the excitement she forced her sunbonnet onto his head. When they regained their feet, the sunbonnet disguised him in the crowd. She got him safely away and into the hands of friends.

It was now 1860. Harriet made one more trip into Maryland, but her friends up and down the routes were fearful for her safety. When John Brown had been captured, lists of sympathizers had been seized with him. The danger was now sharpened and intensified.

But she continued to make her way safely. William Still in Philadelphia had hidden his record book, but on a loose sheet of paper he noted, "Arrived from Dorcester Co. 1860, Harriet Tubman's last trip to Maryland," and the names of her passengers.

Her friends hurried Harriet to Canada. They were convinced she was in extreme danger. Lincoln had just been elected, war was inevitable.

But Harriet could not stay in Canada. She knew too much to be idle. Her friend Governor Andrews of Massachusetts urgently recommended that the army use her as a scout, a spy, a nurse—wherever she was most needed.

The Union forces had taken the Sea Islands off the coast of Georgia. Slaves were spilling onto these islands claiming their freedom. Sick, desperate, starving, many bearing wounds inflicted by their owners as they fled— someone had to care for them.

In a dirty ramshackled room called a hospital, Harriet nursed them as best she could. Medical care in the army was practically unknown, despite the persistent efforts of Dorothea Dix and Elizabeth Blackwell.

Dysentery was sweeping the hospital. Harriet went into the woods and found the roots and herbs which cured dysentery. She brewed them, administered the brew, controlled the epidemic. Then she made pies and root beer to sell, and with the money bought food and supplies for her patients.

When the first Negro regiment, commanded by her old Boston friend, Thomas Wentworth Higginson, paraded into the town, she broke into tears. Men who had been slaves six weeks before now wore the uniform of Union soldiers and marched to the music of a white band playing the great antislavery marching song, "John Brown's Body."

She was asked to join the regiment as a scout. She went on several raiding missions which attacked enemy installations and brought out nearly eight hundred slaves.

For two years she served with the army, providing invaluable assistance. When the war came to an end, she was nursing once more at Fortress Monroe.

With the passage of the Thirteenth Amendment abolishing slavery, Harriet knew one phase of her life had ended and another begun. Women must have the vote!

She clamored for women's rights as cleverly as she had worked for Negro freedom. The freed slaves also concerned her; they must have education and jobs. She thought of a dozen ways to raise money for their schools.

She needed money for herself as well, for the Government had refused her a pension in spite of all the work she had done with the army. Her parents had died, her home in Auburn had become a way station for the poor and forsaken. The people of Auburn knew and admired her. Neighbors helped generously. An admirer wrote her biography and gave her the money from the royalties. She received $1200 from the sales.

Harriet never became an "old woman," though she lived to be ninety-two. Her interest in and work for the sick, the poor, and the homeless kept her young and vital. A new generation heard the stories of her courage and exploits, the love that had led her to help the enslaved and abandoned.

When she died the town of Auburn erected a monument in her honor. On the day that the bronze tablet was unveiled, the city's flags were flown at half-mast.

IN MEMORY OF HARRIET TUBMAN

. . .

CALLED THE MOSES OF HER PEOPLE.
WITH RARE COURAGE SHE LED OVER
THREE HUNDRED NEGROES UP FROM
SLAVERY TO FREEDOM
AND RENDERED INVALUABLE SERVICE
AS NURSE AND SPY.
WITH IMPLICIT TRUST IN GOD
SHE OVERCAME EVERY OBSTACLE.

. . . . .

THIS TABLET IS ERECTED
BY THE CITIZENS OF AUBURN.

SIX

Mary
Baker Eddy

"The voice of God in behalf of the African slave was still echoing in our land, when the voice of the herald of [a] new crusade sounded the keynote of universal freedom, asking a fuller acknowledgment of the rights of man as a Son of God, demanding that the fetters of sin, sickness, and death be stricken from the human mind. . . . Discerning the rights of man we cannot fail to foresee the doom of all oppression."

T HESE ringing words ran counter to all religious and educational belief of the time. But to many they were the logical development of this nineteenth century world, alive with the ferment of freedom and of ideas. They were written by a woman named Mary Baker Eddy. In the years ahead she was to become the only American woman to found a great religious organization as well as a famous international daily newspaper, *The Christian Science Monitor.*

All the women in this book have been concerned with ideas. All tried, in one way or another, to break the preconceptions that held the human race in bondage. Mary Baker Eddy took the most daring step of all. She challenged the very texture of thinking and of humanity's whole concept of itself.

Mary Baker was born in New Hampshire in the same year as Harriet Tubman and Elizabeth Blackwell—1821. She too was a child of that passionate protest of independence which claimed the right of every individual to address his conscience freely. She foresaw much that modern thinking now accepts, particularly the psychological nature of cause and effect.

Not everyone may agree with her ideas, but few today will deny her greatness or the far-reaching effects of her challenging ideas.

Mary Baker was the youngest of six children. Her father, Mark, was a prosperous New Hampshire farmer working his two hundred acres of upland near Bow. He was typical of his time and place: hard-working, conservative, stern. His ancestors had come from England in 1634 looking for religious freedom.

Mark Baker was a fond father though far from indulgent. He was proud of his sons who had the intellectual curiosity which promised a great future in a new nation struggling for its own identity. His daughters, he had no doubt, would follow the best pattern of marriage and secure homes.

Mary was a very pretty child, she was also gentle, tender, and much loved but with great inner strength that was evident even then. She seemed to draw in with the air the feeling that integrity was more important than happiness.

A one-room schoolhouse provided instruction in reading, writing, and arithmetic for which the children walked miles along the dirt roads. One particular morning a group of children stood very quietly by the open school door. Something unpleasant was about to happen, as they knew very well when they saw a tall girl, the school bully, walking slowly along the road with something in her hands. They could tell by the way she walked that she meant trouble. All of them, boys as well as girls, dreaded what she would do. The teacher had not arrived, so they were at the girl's mercy.

As she came through the door the room was very still. A group retreated to the opposite end of the room and remained huddled and quiet. They saw she had a hollowed-out cucumber filled with dirty water. She held it above her head in triumph. With a gleam in her eyes she said, "Everyone of you must take a drink from this cucumber."

No one stirred. As the girl advanced Mary moved out of the group and stood in her path. Mary was eight years old at the time, not very well known to her schoolmates because she was often sick and absent.

Now she stood, half the size of the other girl, her eyes disconcertingly large, intensely blue, and said in a small calm voice, "You shall not touch one of them."

"Get out of my way!" cried the tall girl, splashing a little of the dirty water, "or I will knock you over."

The children gasped, but what happened was enough to make them open their mouths even wider. Mary did not move and suddenly the school bully put down her cucumber, threw her arms around Mary, and kissed her. "You're a brave little rascal!" she cried with a laugh.

Mary's mother was a gentle person, who ran her large household with efficiency. Mother and daughter had an understanding of each other which ran very deep. But let no one doubt who was master. Mark Baker ruled with a firm hand.

His authority was absolute, and there was much about Mary which disturbed him. She was unlike his other children, who were strong, competent, with no hidden subtleties. Mary, was also filled with compassion for weak things. Her brother Albert found her one evening crouch-

ing by the pigsty singing to the piglets because she thought
they needed comfort. She fussed about the horses during
the winter cold, about the ducks when the pond froze. In
her father's opinion she read too much; she was far too
impressionable; she had too many private thoughts for a
little girl.

Although she did not know it, she was living in a
time when thoughtful people were challenging the solidity of matter. In Boston, Ralph Waldo Emerson was suggesting that material things were merely the symbols
of spiritual facts. Theodore Parker, the great Unitarian
minister, was shocking orthodox sense by asserting that it
was not the Jesus who had died eighteen hundred
years before who saved but "the Christ we form in our
hearts and live out in our daily lives."

"Idealist" was the word used for such thinkers. "Tran-
scendentalist" was another word. In any case the philosophic questions they raised were all suggesting that the
solidity of matter was neither the beginning nor the end
of existence, and that moral and physical freedom might
perhaps be found only when this hard surface was
pierced.

Even Abraham Lincoln wrote: "Happy day . . . when all
matter subjected, mind, all conquering mind shall live
and move, the monarch of the world."

These were solitary voices, but they were affecting the
subtle mutation of thought, and we must understand them
a little in order to gain perspective on all the women in
this book, and especially Mary Baker.

The Bakers were churchgoers. The Congregational
Church was the church of New England; it was strict and
Calvinistic. The Bible was the foundation of almost every
home, read aloud twice a day. The Old Testament was

favored and its harsh language was used as a lash against sinners and as a warning even to the righteous.

This orthodox thinking produced some great men and women. It also produced some of the worst enslavement possible to the mind and to society.

Attempts at social reforms were usually opposed vehemently by the churches. To William Lloyd Garrison, at one point, the orthodox churches were a more dangerous enemy to the abolition of slavery than were the slave masters.

Prudence Crandall and Harriet Tubman found that the "inferiority" of the Negro received immense support from the churches. Many doors were closed to Elizabeth Cady Stanton and Elizabeth Blackwell because they fought the churches' contention that women were inferior to men—a conviction based on the text from Genesis II saying Eve had been created after Adam. Dorothea Dix found that efforts to ease the condition of the poor and insane often met resistance because the churches taught that God inflicted suffering for a mysterious reason not to be questioned by man.

Although the Quakers had rejected the dogma of predestination, they did agree on the inevitability of suffering. Although the Unitarians had fought many of the harsh Calvinist tenets, the notion of a God of vengeance still lay heavily on the human heart.

As a child, Mary Baker could simply not accept these bitter doctrines. To her, life itself must be the expression of a loving, active, useful principle or human activity was worth nothing.

Almost everything she did from the time she was twelve years old was to find the reason and proof of this conviction.

It was hard for Mark Baker to find fault with a child who believed God talked to her. Yet he was disturbed when he realized that the talk was of care and forgiveness, rather than of wrath and punishment.

Their conflict of ideologies came to a head when Mary reached the age of twelve. A Calvinist child was then supposed to show herself sound in doctrine by an outward profession of faith. Mark Baker called Mary into the parlor for examination. She gravely faced him and did what no other child of his had thought or dared to do. She began to argue.

How could she believe in a God who "saved" only a few and condemned the others without a sign of mercy? She could only love a God who was himself a loving father to all his children.

Mark Baker was outraged and demanded that she take back her words. She shook her head, her face white under the strain. Mary, despite her gentleness, was very much her father's daughter. When opposed she was able to show a will as powerful as his own. The struggle between them went on for days, for neither would yield. The whole house lay under the shadow of Mark Baker's anger and shock. At last Mary collapsed. Her father was filled with fear. He could not bear the thought of losing this child who was so like him, so courageous. He rushed out of the house, hitched a horse to the wagon, and careened down the hill for a doctor.

"Where are you going in such a hurry?" a neighbor called out to him. Mark drove on with a stricken cry. "Mary is dying!"

A fever, the family doctor said on examining the child. He knew Mark Baker too well not to guess the cause. She must be left in peace. Mark Baker, chastened, left Mary to the care of her mother.

Abigail Baker seldom opposed her husband, but to Mary she said that God's love would give her healing and guidance.

As for Mark Baker he recognized his own strength in her, and never again opposed her on the ground of conscience. It was Albert, her oldest brother, who gave her practical understanding and love. He was fascinated by her curiosity and tossed her smatterings of his own education so that she might know "something more each day than the day before." Any mental exercise delighted her, and in school a philosophic question was put to her one day: "If an orange were peeled, its juice squeezed out, and its seed and pulp destroyed, what would be left?" No one could think of an answer beyond suggesting, "Nothing." Mary ventured to say, "The *thought* of the orange would be left."

When she was twenty she fell in love and married. By now she was slender and attractive with a heavy mass of chestnut-colored hair and the remarkable eyes which have been described as gray, blue, violet.

The name of her young husband was George Washington Glover. His sister had married Mary's brother Samuel. George was a dashing Bostonian, romantically handsome, with a debonair manner. He was a building contractor and shortly before his marriage had established a profitable business in Charleston, South Carolina—a stronghold of slavery. George did not give much thought to slavery one way or the other, but Mary was appalled.

She tried hard not to think about it, to enjoy her new life as a young married woman, but she could not maintain the pretense of indifference. She was greatly relieved when George received a contract to supply the material for the building of a cathedral in Haiti for they could leave Charleston. George invested most of his money in building materials and took Mary with him to Wilmington, North Carolina, to supervise the shipping. It was an exciting adventure for Mary, who had the added delight of knowing that she was pregnant. Without warning, all this joy was struck down. George became deathly sick with malaria, and the doctor would not let Mary, in her condition, go near him. Within a few days he was dead.

Mary found herself virtually destitute. All of George's capital had been in his supplies for Haiti and, during the week of his illness, the supplies had been stolen. Nothing was left but two or three slaves who had been given to George in payment. She would neither keep them nor sell them, but set them free. Although this gave them no legal protection, it was the best she could do. She returned to the home of her parents, sick and penniless.

No one believed that she would survive the birth of her child. When a boy, named George after his father, was born in September, 1844, she was too ill to nurse him. The baby was given for nursing to a neighbor who had just lost her child.

Mary grew weaker. She could not find the will to rouse herself. The baby, growing into a noisy, energetic child, could only be handled by a family servant, Mahala Sanborn. When Mary's mother, whom she loved dearly, suddenly died, life seemed to lose all its purpose.

But Mary's spirit was very stubborn and refused to yield to illness and depression. All her latent convictions came to her support. She became more and more confident that suffering was evil, that since the world did not know what to do about it, the world had rationalized it as God-sent.

She struggled back to some semblance of health because she knew she must find a way to support her child or be dependent on her family. She had many suitors at this time, but her streak of independence made her long to prove her self-reliance. Mark Baker was impatient with her boisterous young son. This created a strain between Mary and her father and she renewed her efforts to earn a living. In addition to the handicap of being a woman she was also very frail, with a sickness of the spine. She taught school, she sold some of her poems and essays, but this was the most she could do.

Mark Baker, a man of bursting health and energy, decided after a short time to marry again. Although Mary liked his new wife, she did not wish to remain in their house. Mary's wealthy sister, Abigail Tilton, offered to give her a home, but since she had a sickly son she refused to have Mary's energetic George.

Mary had to kiss her son good-by and send him off with Mahala, who had married and gone to live on a farm forty miles away. This depressed her deeply. To get well, to become self-supporting so that she could recover her son—this was all she wanted, but she was asking a miracle.

She had a vague, persistent sense that "miracle" was not a word meaning "impossible." The Bible abounded in miracles, treating them as though they were natural occurrences. And why not? How little was known of natural force. Why should any experience, diverging from a familiar pattern, be immediately labeled unnatural? Why should people not suppose (as a philosopher, Richard Hildreth, had written a few years earlier) that miracles might "occur in conformity to some law hitherto unknown: and instead of resting in wondering and superstitious ignorance, the whole science of the age would be turned to discover what the law was."

As the months of separation from her son wore on, Mary searched for a solution to her desperate problem. Often discouraged, she would not admit defeat. But hope was becoming very frail when Dr. Daniel Patterson suddenly came into her life. His energy and enthusiasm were like a breath of air.

He was a relative of her stepmother, a large, cheerful, handsome man who exuded a sense of well-being. Everyone felt that his overflowing vigor, his love for Mary, would solve her problems. As a professional man, a dentist, it was assumed he could support her and he promised that she should have her son.

But the marriage proved to be a miserably unhappy step for both of them. Daniel refused to let George come to them until Mary was strong enough to care for him. He fully expected that she would recover quickly under his brisk and cheerful nursing. When her illness grew worse on learning that she must continue to wait for her son, he was bewildered.

There was no doubt Daniel loved her deeply, but Mary was not a woman he could understand. In fact she bewildered him completely. All his good-natured and easy-going weaknesses took over. He proved to be a poor provider and an unreliable husband. He was away from home a great deal, partly because he was an itinerant dentist, traveling from town to town with his bag of instruments, partly because his temperament was restless.

In 1855 they moved to North Groton, New Hampshire, a lonely and beautiful village on a mountain. Mary's son lived nearby with his foster parents, the Sanborns. For a time Mary was happy. George came to her for some of his lessons. Then suddenly, without warning, the Sanborns left for Minnesota, taking George with them.

Whether this was their decision or Daniel's Mary did not know; she knew only that her young son was lost now forever.

This great, prime disappointment, linked with her husband's good-natured failures, made these the blackest days of her life. Her world was filled with jangled nerves and unanswered questions. She had no books except the Bible and a volume on homeopathy in which Daniel was interested. Mary began to study it.

Homeopathy, very popular at the time, was a method of treating disease by drugs, given in minute doses, which produced in a healthy person symptoms similar to the disease.

Her inner questioning went on, day and night. Homeopathy seemed to confirm her impression that it was the faith in the drugs which healed, not the attenuated drugs. Spiritualism and mesmerism, also popular in New England at this time, suggested to her ranging curiosity that mind and spirit might, in fact, be more powerful than matter.

These were all tentative, exploratory thoughts, which she in turn examined and discarded. Yet all served to hint at the mental nature of objective phenomena.

When the Civil War broke out Mary was still bedridden, still longing to be free. She wrote to General Benjamin Butler, who had taken a radical position protecting slaves who escaped to the Union forces (most generals sent them back to their masters). She thanked him in the name of "thousands of my sex" and insisted that his courageous stand would be vindicated, freedom given "to black as well as white—men, women, and children . . . You hold freedom to be the normal condition of those made in God's image."

Her husband was chaffing for the excitement of war. Early in 1862 he was commissioned by the governor of New Hampshire to distribute money raised to assist those beleaguered Southerners who refused to support the Confederacy. (It was these people whom Jefferson Davis said won the war for the Union.) It was a delicate and very dangerous task. It is not surprising that he was taken prisoner.

Confederate prisons were hell-holes. Mary did everything she could to arrange for his release. She wrote to the Secretary of War and to Franklin Pierce, the former President who had been her brother's friend, but not until the end of the year was Daniel able to accomplish his own daring escape.

During this time Mary lived in the little backwoods world of North Groton, with no one to talk to except her devoted servant girl Myra, who was blind. Both were trapped by physical infirmities. Mary believed an answer lay close at hand. Moses, Elijah, and Jesus had healed as naturally as the sun rose. How? Try as she did she could not find an answer.

Through the newspapers Mary learned of a faith healer named Phineas P. Quimby who lived in Portland, Maine. He had attracted much attention and she longed to have his help. She thought about him constantly and presently neither lack of money nor weakness could hold her back. One day in October, 1862, she appeared at Quimby's door.

Quimby was a bright, energetic little man of sixty, enormously kind and sympathetic. He took Mary in, and before the week was out she was able to walk up to the dome of the City Hall, 180 steps. She was jubilant. He, in his kind way, was delighted.

Perhaps her tensions had merely been relaxed, perhaps hope had given her a fresh impetus, but she was convinced that Quimby had discovered something which she must understand.

In many ways his theories were very original, but in other ways they merely reflected the current popularity of "mind over matter," the control of physical cause and effect by physical manipulation and mental effort. His method was to explain to his patient how grief or fear "congested" into lung ailments or cancer or heart trouble. He was an illiterate man, but he had worked for ten years to develop the ideas and vocabulary which explained what he believed. Gradually he became convinced that he was healing in the way Jesus had healed.

He and Mary talked by the hour. She too was convinced that he had a divine power. His confidence was like an electric force to which she responded and which she tried to link with her spiritual concepts.

They talked on two different levels: Quimby's ideas were focused on "spiritualizing" and controlling matter, while Mary sought an understanding of purely spiritual causes, completely free of all physical control. Yet each was caught by the other's ideas.

He gave her the notes he had made, his broken and poorly spelled efforts to formulate his theories. She gave them back to him with written comments of her own. Quimby was one of those rare people, a truly unselfish man. His work was his life, but he was as interested in Mary's development as in his own. When, one day in his absence, she "healed" a man who had been seriously injured, Quimby was as pleased as she.

It was a profound experience for Mary. Quimby had believed that his healings were the result of some mysterious law of suggestion. Mary had insisted that they were the effect of a divine power not fully understood. Now she must find the truth.

All the steps she had taken were clear. When the manager of the hotel had asked her help for the injured man, panic had overwhelmed her at first. But a surge of compassion had put words in her mouth, and she had insisted on the power and presence of a compassionate God. The man had walked.

How? How? She had turned with all her heart to a loving source of life in which she believed. Was a simple rule of healing to be found in this?

She was happy and confident for the first time in many years. It was at this point that Daniel returned. He had escaped from the Confederates and arrived in Portland thin, ill, and in need of her. And Mary was healthy and able to give him a home.

They went to Lynn, Massachusetts.

Bitter disappointments soon intruded on her happiness and drained her strength. Daniel was restless and roaming but without his old charm. Her illness returned. She wrote desperately to Quimby, but try as he did he seemed unable to help her as he had in the past.

The kind, confused little man kept invading her thoughts. In January, 1866, he died. The emptiness left by his death forced her to search more deeply her own developing thoughts. As the years went on and her spiritual assurance grew, she could look back on this period and see that Quimby's healings had represented a tremendous personal force which was quite contrary to the profound and universal law that came as her revelation. She could see, in addition, that his manipulation of thought was dangerous to the free spirit of man.

One February night she was returning with friends from a Good Templars meeting when she slipped on the ice and fell so violently that she lost consciousness. Her friends carried her to a nearby house and a doctor was called. He found that she had received a concussion and that her spine had been injured again. He warned that she might not recover, or, if she did, remain a helpless invalid. The next day she was still unconscious, but on the third day she roused enough to ask her friends to give her a Bible and leave her alone.

The moment had come when she must prove that law of healing on which her faith was based. She knew that the Bible said: "Behold I set before you this day death or life, blessing or cursing. Choose." She turned to Matthew 9:2 which she had read and thought about many times—the account of Jesus healing the palsied man.

Mary's friends were sitting in helpless anxiety in the next room. Suddenly the door opened and Mary walked in. In their consternation they believed she was a ghost. She convinced them she was alive. She was smiling. She was well.

One friend gasped that this was a miracle, but fear and dismay were their principal emotions. The challenge was out of all proportion to their experience.

For Mary life now had a purpose. She saw that she would have to devote all her thoughts and her ability in order to grasp the full meaning of what had taken place. For twenty years she had been searching. Now she was convinced that she had found a workable proposition "that Mind is all and matter is naught as the leading fact in Mind-science."

That capital M was the key to her meaning. She saw Mind as synonymous with God. To her the "true idea of the infinite Godhead" expressed itself in additional synonyms: Life, Truth, Love, Spirit, Soul, Principle—a definition so broad in its scope that many physicists and astronomers have begun to utilize some of these terms—Mind and Principle, especially—as expressive of the cause of the universe.

All this came much later, however. The next few weeks demanded all her courage. Her friends were solicitous and incredulous. She herself almost faltered, but she could not give up her growing conviction that Jesus' words, "Go ye into all the world and heal the sick," were meant for every Christian.

As she held doggedly, tremulously, to the faith born of her experience, she took the next step: if the knowledge of healing had been lost, it could be found again. Gradually she began to realize that by insisting upon a rule of healing she was moving far beyond the scope of Quimby. She did not need Quimby. She needed only God. "Since God is All, there is no room for His unlikeness. God, Spirit, alone created all and called it good. Therefore evil being contrary to God . . . cannot be the product of God."

This was a radical idealism, to be sure, going much farther than any philosopher. But "the time for thinkers has come," she wrote in an early edition of *Science and Health*, "and the time for revolutions, ecclesiastic and social must come. Truth, independent of doctrines and time-honored systems, stands at the threshold of history."

It was obvious that she had to follow where her teeming thoughts were leading her.

The next three years were lonely and desperate. Yet, later on, she recalled them as "sweet, calm, and buoyant with hope." This is probably far nearer the essential truth than the homeless, poverty-stricken days indicated.

She had separated from Daniel Patterson and would presently be obliged to divorce him. Living a hand-to-mouth existence, she moved from one boardinghouse to another. She had become a woman possessed by a single idea, driven by the need to explore her discovery to its source.

Her only friends were factory workers of Lynn who lived in the boardinghouses. She was an enigma to them. Obviously a lady, attractive, intelligent, educated—yet all she talked and reasoned about was the message of healing which Jesus had brought.

But these factory workers were sons and daughters of those same simple people who had helped William Lloyd Garrison launch a moral revolution, who had formed philosophy and reading circles in their factories. *Ideas* were not foreign to them. Many listened to Mary with deep curiosity and attention. Others were bored. The interested ones multiplied. She was a born teacher.

Some asked her to heal them, and she did—with an almost unbroken record of success. Some thought her mentally unbalanced. One who had listened went to the superintendent of an insane asylum, saying that Mary should be examined. The superintendent came to inquire for himself. Instead of talking about herself, she discussed his method of caring for his mental patients, and when he left he thanked her for the help her ideas had given him in the difficult world of mental therapy.

In the course of her wanderings Mary went to stay with Mrs. Nathaniel Webster in Amesbury, Massachusetts. Mrs. Webster was an ardent spiritualist. She could not grasp Mary's purpose and thought Mary was writing a revision of the Bible, but she loved her and welcomed her.

At this time Mary was attempting to set down a com-

mentary on the scriptures which would explain as pene-
tratingly as possible what she felt her discovery to be.
In the summer Mrs. Webster's son returned to the house
with his family. He disapproved of his mother's uncon-
ventional ideas and took a particular dislike to Mary. He
ordered her out, and when she objected, he put her
out bodily, bag and baggage.

Mary sat on the stoop, the rain pouring down in buck-
ets, not knowing in what direction to turn. Timidity, self-
distrust, friendlessness—she knew them all; and sitting
where the pouring rain splashed on her skirt, she must
have needed all the courage in the world.

Another boarder, Richard Kennedy, who had taken
her side, joined her on the dark lonely stoop. He was a
young man in his twenties who had been absorbing
Mary's ideas. He suggested they go to a relative of his,
Miss Sarah Bagley.

Miss Bagley took them both in—one would take in any
strays on such a night—and as the days went on she
asked Mary so many questions she might properly be
called a student.

Richard Kennedy, as eager and curious as Miss Bagley,
advanced so rapidly in his grasp of Mary's teachings that
in two years he left his factory job to devote all his time
to healing. In 1870 they rented rooms over a kinder-
garten in Lynn. It was planned that Richard should be
the practitioner and Mary the teacher. A sign was put
up to announce the fact, and presently both Richard and
Mary were working all the time. Mary offered a course of
twelve lessons for $300. To her delight twelve people
enrolled as students.

The sessions were argumentative but, on Mary's part,
absolutely firm. From the very beginning she spoke and
wrote with utter authority, although her ideas were

being freshly illuminated as she went on. The logic of her own insight compelled her to see that truth, by its very nature, was demonstrable, hence scientific. Therefore the truth, or science, of the creative Principle which made man and the whole universe must be demonstrable in its own terms. This was elemental logic. Ignorance might obscure this fact but only in the way that a mathematical equation could confuse and mislead unless the correct factors were used.

She was convinced that a true healing as a work of science had to be wholly spiritual, and that any material aid was not only unnecessary but must be avoided. She told Richard that all his "laying on of hands" had to stop. In dismay and rebellion he left her and went off on his own.

A few of her followers stayed with her, meeting together on Sunday, performing cures which seemed to startle them as much as the people cured.

Mary was spending most of her time writing a book. Every fine day she carried her Bible and writing materials to a rock by the seaside where she could be alone. A title for her book eluded her but it finally came "in the silence of the night . . . *Science and Health.*"

A few weeks later someone showed her a translation by Wycliffe of the New Testament. There were the words "science and health" which in the King James' version are translated "knowledge of salvation."

"Knowledge of salvation" . . . to Mary these words meant freedom.

She could not find a publisher willing to undertake the risk of a book designed to "reinstate the lost element of healing." Money had to be raised by her friends, and fifteen hundred copies were printed privately.

A few newspapers treated the book quite well in reviews,

but most simply ignored it. It was then that her energetic band of students traveled from door to door selling
the book. Advertising space was bought in the newspapers. Copies were sent to libraries and universities and
to prominent people. *Science and Health* began to be circulated by enthusiastic readers who lent the book to
others, until the number of readers far exceeded the number of copies sold.

Very gradually recognition of the book began to grow
until one day Mary found herself holding a letter from
the philosopher and teacher Bronson Alcott, friend of
Emerson and father of Louisa who wrote *Little Women*.

In his diary he had written some years before, "I imagine that it will be possible, yea certain, that the miracles, so-called [of Jesus] . . . shall be made as common
facts, the necessary and natural results of spritual law."

Now he wrote to Mary: "I hail with joy your voice,
speaking an assured word for God and immortality, and my
joy is heightened that these words are woman's divin-
ings." He visited her a few days later and called her work
a reaffirmation "in modern phrase" of "the Christian revelation." He saw her as "one of the fair saints."

Her followers were healing whoever asked for help, and
what they occasionally failed to do, Mary did for them.
They were oblivious to the cries of "charlatan—
hypnotist."

In 1876 The Christian Science Association was formed
to hold regular weekly meetings in Lynn and sometimes
in Boston, Roxbury, and Salem. One of Mary's keenest
students was Asa Gilbert Eddy. He had been healed by
her of a lingering infection. This healing so impressed
Gilbert Eddy that he promptly enrolled in one of Mary's
classes. By the end of the course he was ready to set up

practice. He was the first to call himself by the title, "Christian Science practitioner."

Gilbert Eddy proved to be an enormous help to Mary, for she was, at this time, working night and day, healing, teaching, and bringing order into a swiftly expanding movement. In these early days she learned much from trial and error. Feeling her way, she was trying to find new and more exact means of explaining Christian Science and at the same time provide clear guidelines for Christian Scientists.

Gilbert Eddy was a calm, energetic man, very competent, very swift to grasp what was needed. He handled practical matters skillfully. Since Christian Science was spreading with extraordinary speed, these talents were almost indispensable to Mary. To find a man with these qualities, who could keep pace with her and whom she respected, filled her heart. On New Year's Day, 1877, they were married.

By now Christian Science was creating a great commotion. Although it had relatively few adherents, its enemies gave it a prominence it might not have reached for many years. Sometimes it seemed as though every rational and irrational difficulty was put in Mary's way. A climax came with a mysterious and involved accusation against Gilbert Eddy of conspiracy to murder. Gilbert was vindicated when it was proved he was the victim of collusion, but cruel and unfounded charges made the enemies of Christian Science jubilant. They anticipated a rapid dissolution of the movement.

But the turmoil, the constant challenges, served to clarify objectives for Mary. She had virtually no precedent to go on. Some students proved to be her worst enemies. They wanted to sensationalize Christian Science in order to catch the public fancy. She was determined that Christian Science must develop in an orderly and logical way.

The small group in Lynn, stumbling, righting itself, shining out like early Christians, was still too preoccupied with the present to think much of the future. Mary's expectation that all sects of Christians would work together and accept literally Jesus' command "Go ye into all the world and heal the sick" had received many a setback. Now she saw that Christian Scientists would need their own church in order to maintain their identity.

She acted quickly. A church charter was obtained and the Church of Christ, Scientist, was organized under the state laws. Two years later she was given a charter for a Metaphysical College where she could handle the rapidly growing demand for instruction.

She had every reason to feel that the worst was over. Even those who felt that they knew more than she and went off on their own carried the startling message of a science of healing.

Then, as had happened so often in her life, the one nearest her died. Gilbert Eddy, for no apparent reason, sickened and was gone.

She blamed herself bitterly for having been so busy that she had not insisted on helping and curing him herself. She was filled with grief and she fled to a friend in Vermont.

The students who had been left to care for things in Boston were badly shaken. But within a few days she had regained control of herself. "For I do believe in God's supremacy over evil and this gives me peace."

By now the orthodox churches were beginning to bring to bear the full weight of their displeasure. This indicated, for better or worse, that Christian Science had attained a strong position. Newspapers all over the country wakened to a dramatic force in their midst.

Both churches and newspapers attacked Mary because she was a woman. "This is woman's hour!" was her spirited answer. "The conclusion cannot now be pushed that women have no rights that a man is bound to respect. . . . It is the pulpit and press, clerical robes and the prohibiting of free speech that cradles and covers the sins of the world. . . . The cry of the colored slave has scarcely been heard and hushed when another form of inhumanity lifts its hydra head to forge anew the old fetters to shackle conscience, stop free speech, slander, vilify . . . and refuse the victim a solitary vindication in this most unprecedented warfare."

Yet the only vindication she sought was in lives renewed, spiritually and physically. Her persistent, unwavering vision sharpened her energy. She was now a woman in her sixties. She preached almost every Sunday and lectured every Thursday. At the same time she planned a magazine, *The Christian Science Journal* which virtually single-handed she brought to publication in April, 1883.

For the next eight years she lived the lives of a dozen women, and at the same time tried to have some privacy from the crowds of the curious, sympathetic or hostile. In these eight years Christian Science began to spread all over the world. This gave rise to even greater opposition from the orthodox clergy; the doctors were not as angry as the theologians.

A particularly virulent attack was made on her by a celebrated clergyman. She asked the right to reply. She was allowed ten minutes in Tremont Temple. The building was packed. She began with a statement of faith.

"I believe in God as the Supreme Being. I know not what the person of omnipotence and omnipresence is, or what the infinite includes; therefore I worship that of which I can conceive—first as a loving Father and Mother; then, as thought ascends the scale of being to diviner consciousness, God becomes to me . . . divine Principle."

In the nine minutes left her, she told what Christian Science was *not*. *Not* one mind acting on another through thought transference, not "a remedy of faith alone" but faith linked to understanding. And she quoted the Icelandic translation of the creation of man: "He created man in the image and likeness of Mind."

She had, of course, gained powerful friends as well as powerful enemies. Edward Everett Hale, the most influential clergyman in Boston at that time, wrote: "She has taught me more truth in twenty minutes than I have learned in years." And Wendell Phillips, who had been Garrison's right hand, said, "Had I young blood in my veins I would help that woman."

These men responded to the qualities she shared with all the women in this book—a vivid idealism, immense courage, and a spiritual valor which embraced the needs of the whole world.

She was quick to recognize that the religion she was working so hard to illuminate could degenerate into a personality cult unless its purity was kept intact. The proof and the climax came when she went to Chicago in June, 1888, to meet Christian Scientists from all over the country. When the Chicago newspapers learned this they made headline news of the event. The Central Music Hall which normally seated eight hundred was packed by four thousand.

Mary had not intended to make a speech but circumstances compelled her. Her spontaneous words were called the best statement on the meaning of Christian Science ever made from a public platform. They aroused such excitement that the audience rushed onto the stage, weeping, cheering, and scrambling to touch her.

She was deeply shocked. She returned to Boston with sharp words: "Christian Science is not forwarded by these methods." She saw that the movement might be endangered by growing too fast.

She closed the college, dissolved the organization, and suggested that each of the church members "return to his place of labor to work out individually and alone, for himself and for others, the sublime ends of human life."

She went back to New Hampshire. She bought land in Concord and modernized a house which stood only a few miles from the place of her birth, overlooking the hills of her childhood.

It was difficult for others to understand this daring move with its brave inspiration. Her students seemed to have been left adrift. Outsiders did not realize that she was requiring every Christian Scientist to decide exactly how important his religion was to himself and how he could stand alone. What she saw satisfied her and confirmed her feeling that she should remain in Concord. She stayed there from 1899 to 1908.

It was a period of intense thought and activity for her and those around her. She demanded of her household a dedication as intense as her own and offered in return her compassion and her warm sense of humor. No one close to Mary could help but respond, for her insights revealed the possibility of a world without limitations.

As time went on she urged and helped her students

to build a church in Boston to be called the Mother Church. Its members would be drawn from Christian Scientists all over the world. Because she realized that such a development could raise again her old apprehensions about organization, she coordinated all the practical rules of governing which her experience had taught her. These rules became a Church Manual, a book of remarkable insight, protecting the church in almost every way from personal cliques and casual development.

One step she considered very important—to protect Christian Science churches from any sense of rivalry resulting from overly ambitious pastors. The King James' version of the Bible and *Science and Health with Key to the Scriptures* were "ordained" pastor over the Mother Church. She added later to a friend, "The voice of God, not human views, should preach to humanity . . . If Christian Science lacked the proof of its goodness and utility it would destroy itself, for it rests alone on demonstration."

Twice during this decade of the 1890s the Massachusetts legislature attempted to put through a medical bill restraining Christian Science. Each time it was defeated. Unexpected supporters appeared. For example, William James, the great philosopher, and himself a doctor, argued the right of spiritual healing. And Garrison's son, William, made a strong appeal for the rights of Christian Scientists.

By 1900 branch churches were developing at such a rate that Mark Twain—a former enemy who had become a friend—insisted a new one appeared every four days. In vivid words Mrs. Eddy summarized the work already done and waiting to be done: "Truth cannot be stereotyped. It unfoldeth forever."

By 1902 it was clear that the Boston church was far too small for its needs. Within four years an extension double in size was built, and during the week of its dedication Mary Baker Eddy was the most discussed woman in the world, if the newspapers can be trusted. She was now eighty-four years old and looked very much younger. She was slim, quick, and graceful. Her eyes were still the extraordinary luminous ones of her youth. She was a woman known and seen by thousands. When a savage attack was suddenly hurled at her it became a sensation.

The attack had been carefully planned by Joseph Pulitzer, the powerful newspaper owner who provided the means and the money. Why he did this was never clear, perhaps to increase circulation.

The Pulitzer papers charged that she was not only incompetent to manage her affairs but was so senile that she had fallen into the hands of an unscrupulous group who were exploiting her fame and wealth.

Concord was suddenly overrun with Pulitzer reporters. They had been instructed to get the "truth" provided it met the standards of sensationalism. Her own son, who had become a mining prospector in the West, was drawn into the case against her. He joined out of ignorance and solicitude, accepting false evidence that she needed protecting. The attacks served one purpose, however. They allowed a remarkably vivid woman to attest to her own identity.

She did it with humor and courtesy. A psychiatrist who had been assigned by the court summed it up: "For a woman of her age I do not hesitate to say that she is physically and mentally phenomenal. . . . In her ordinary conversation she is witty and a bit satirical, but with a great deal of gentleness in her demeanor."

Arthur Brisbane, who was a famous newspaper editor of the day, came from New York to interview her.

> Mrs. Eddy's face is almost entirely free from wrinkles . . . and the whole expression of her face combines benevolence with great strength of will. Mrs. Eddy has accumulated power in this world. She possesses it, she exercises it, and she knows it. But it is a gentle power, and it is possessed by a gentle, diffident and modest woman.

The judge, lawyers, and court-appointed "Masters" called on Mrs. Eddy at her home in Concord. Whatever was left of the case fell apart during that visit. She answered all questions with her brisk and keen turn of phrase and pointed out, with some amusement, that she was playing host to her own investigators. The charges became more absurd moment by moment.

When the case was dismissed she made only one comment: "When these things cease to bless they will cease to occur."

In January, 1908, she left Concord and returned to Boston. She had one more project, the establishing of a daily newspaper. Its importance may have been underlined by the viciousness of the newspaper attacks on her. Its object, she said, was "to injure no man but to bless all mankind." She called it *The Christian Science Monitor* and it has become one of the few great international newspapers of our time.

On December 3, 1910, she died so quietly that it seemed as though she had merely opened a door and slipped through. On the notepad by her bed she had written these words:

"God is my Life."